YOUth

YOUth

THE YOUNG PERSON'S GUIDE TO STARTING A NONPROFIT

OLIVIA ZHANG

Berrett-Koehler
—— PUBLISHERS

Berrett-Koehler Publishers, Inc.
1333 Broadway, Suite P100
Oakland, CA 94612-1921
(510) 817-2277
bkconnection.com

ORDERING INFORMATION
Quantity sales. Special discounts are available on quantity purchases by corporations, associations, and others. For details, please go to bkconnection.com to see our bulk discounts or contact bookorders@bkpub.com for more information.
Textbook exam/desk copies. Please consult the General FAQ at bkconnection.com.
Bookstore orders for trade or textbook use. For print books, please contact Penguin Random House Publisher Services at customerservice@penguinrandomhouse.com. For ebooks, contact your favorite distributor.

Distributed to the US trade and internationally by Penguin Random House Publisher Services.

The authorized representative in the EU for product safety and compliance is EU Compliance Partner, Pärnu mnt. 139b-14, 11317 Tallinn, Estonia, www.eucompliancepartner.com, +372 5368 65 02.

Berrett-Koehler and the BK logo are registered trademarks of Berrett-Koehler Publishers, Inc.

Printed in the United State of America

Berrett-Koehler books are printed on long-lasting acid-free paper. When it is available, we choose paper that has been manufactured by environmentally responsible processes. These may include using trees grown in sustainable forests, incorporating recycled paper, minimizing chlorine in bleaching, or recycling the energy produced at the paper mill.

Cataloging-in-Publication Data is on file at the Library of Congress.
Library of Congress Control Number: 2025030853
ISBN 9798890571533 paperback | ISBN 9798890571540 pdf | ISBN 9798890571557 epub

First Edition
33 32 31 30 29 28 27 26 25   10 9 8 7 6 5 4 3 2 1

Book production: Happenstance Type-O-Rama
Cover design: Ashley Ingram

For my mother and Ellen Reilly—
the first two people who taught me what
it means to lead with grit and purpose.
You shaped who I am today.

CONTENTS

Introduction 1

1 What Exactly Is a "Nonprofit"? 5

2 The Power of YOUth: Leveraging Your Age 17

3 Planning, Prepping, and Prototyping 29

4 Assembling the Nonprofit Superteam 43

5 Dollars and Dreams 67

6 Branding Yourself and Your Story 77

7 The Ups and the Downs 91

8 Measure It, Scale It 111

Conclusion 121

Toolbox for Changemakers 123

Notes 129

Acknowledgments 131

Index 133

About the Author 143

INTRODUCTION

FROM POLITICAL POLARIZATION TO CLIMATE CHANGE, the world is facing countless challenges. However, a new generation of leaders is stepping up to challenge the status quo, advocate for reform, and make a difference in the lives of others—and **YOU** have the chance to be a part of that movement. It all starts with YOU. What problem keeps YOU up at night? What problems do YOU wish you could do something about? In *YOUth: The Young Person's Guide to Starting a Nonprofit*, I will provide you with tangible steps you can implement as a young person to better your community.

You might be wondering what qualifications I have to be writing this book. After all, I don't have a degree in nonprofit management, nor have I spent decades working in the nonprofit sector. However, I was in your shoes just a few years ago.

Hey! My name is Olivia, and I'm the founder and CEO of Cancer Kids First (CKF), the world's largest youth-led nonprofit aiding kids with cancer. After losing my grandfather and elementary school teacher to cancer within months of each other, I founded CKF at fourteen to honor their legacies and turn my grief into a purpose-driven project. Simply volunteering or fundraising didn't feel like enough—I wanted to address deeper gaps in cancer care, including disparities in treatment quality.

Since 2019, CKF has united 40,500 volunteer members across 80 countries and established 111 chapters. We've donated over $600,000 in resource kits, toys, books, and equipment to 74 hospitals, reaching 10,000 patients in 22 countries. We've hosted 250-plus events and partnered with 39 businesses, including Kendra Scott.

This work led me to serve as the youngest board member on organizations like WEGO Health and World Child Cancer USA. I also founded a nonprofit mentorship network, through which I've helped 187 young leaders build their own organizations—impacting 15,000 people through causes from mental health to STEM access for kids with autism.

Now a Harvard undergraduate studying economics, I've gained further insight into leadership and business. My work has been featured in *People, Business Insider, CBS News, New York Times Upfront*, on the TEDx stage, and more. I was honored as the youngest 2025 L'Oréal Paris Women of Worth, received the 2023 Diana Legacy Award with recognition from Prince William and Prince Harry, named the youngest-ever WEGO Health Top Patient Leader from over 16,000 nominations, and listed in Girls' Life 30 Under 30.

In an effort to share my journey and advice with other young leaders, I began posting nonprofit how-to videos on TikTok in late 2023, growing to 150,000-plus followers and 30 million views. As my nonprofit how-to videos gained traction, I created a concise Google Doc with step-by-step instructions explaining how to start a nonprofit, which received over 400,000 views—but I still get daily requests over social media DMs, texts, and emails for more specific advice. That's why I wrote this book: to share everything I know in one place. Inside, you'll find clear, actionable steps, real stories, and a "Toolbox for Changemakers" to help you launch your own nonprofit journey.

My journey over the past five years with CKF means that I have navigated the challenges of building a mission-driven organization from the ground up, mobilizing volunteers, securing funding, and making a tangible impact, all while balancing school and other commitments. At fourteen, I struggled immensely to find resources to guide me. Luckily, I found mentors who helped me scale effectively, but much of my journey with CKF came from trial and error. Through *YOUth*, my goal is to share the invaluable lessons I learned to make this process smoother for future generations of changemakers—because the future isn't just about youth, it's shaped by YOUth!

1

What Exactly Is a "Nonprofit"?

LET'S START WITH THE VERY BASICS.

What even is a "nonprofit"? What is the difference between a community project and a government-registered nonprofit? What's the difference between a for-profit business and a nonprofit?

Charity organizations exist all throughout the world. There are over 10 million nonprofits worldwide, with close to 1.5 million in the United States alone.[1] Each of these organizations provides individuals with a means of cooperating for the benefit of others, putting their shared aspirations and ideals into practice. The world's 10 million nonprofit organizations strive to heal, shelter, educate, inspire, and grow people of all ages, genders, races, and socioeconomic backgrounds. Nonprofit organizations promote civic engagement and leadership, mend communities, and stimulate economic growth.

From the less fun perspective (aka the legal perspective), the most commonly recognized form of nonprofit organizations is tax-exempt organizations that qualify for tax-exempt status under the US tax code. Each applicable section governing nonprofits offers guidelines for demonstrating why a particular organization is exempt from paying taxes to the federal government. The single most common condition is not distributing profits to benefit "any private shareholder or individual," which is why it is called a nonprofit.[2]

There are over thirty different types of tax-exempt organizations, from those set out in Section 501(c)(4), which are social welfare organizations and volunteer fire companies, to those in Section 501(k), which encompass childcare organizations. Our primary focus is on the magical 501(c)(3). This section of the tax code refers to "public charities," churches and religious institutions, and "private foundations." The main difference between the three is how they get their funding. Public charities, like the name suggests, receive most of their funding from the general public or government. Private foundations, usually founded by a wealthy individual, family, or business, generally have a smaller number of donors who contribute.

Congress also identifies nonprofit organizations as groups of people working toward a common charitable purpose, relieving government burden by serving the community. In turn, the government allows nonprofits to operate without paying income taxes. Tax exemption also makes it easier for nonprofits to raise funds and reinvest surplus revenue into their mission, rather than into owners and shareholders, promoting a culture of giving and supporting the nonprofit model. Under Section 501(c)(3), to remain tax exempt, organizations are required to carry out activities true to their founding purpose, and generally, they are forbidden from performing activities that influence political campaigns or parties.

Still interested in starting a 501(c)(3)? Let's dive in!

Before You Get Started

Ask yourself, "Why do I want to start this nonprofit?" A nonprofit can be a very fulfilling and exciting endeavor, but it may not be the right fit for you. You're required to comply with certain restrictions because you're a tax-exempt organization, your financial information is publicly accessible, and you've got to have the tenacity to push through all-nighters, failures, and other challenges. Consider if you could accomplish your goal in another manner. The following are some other examples of social change projects you can initiate and the reasons why they may be a better fit than starting a nonprofit:

- Volunteering with an existing organization
  - You'd rather contribute than lead.
  - Your passion aligns with an existing mission.
  - You're unsure about long-term commitment.
- Creating a school club
  - Your impact is local or school-wide.
  - You want to test out an idea.
  - You need minimal financial investment or would benefit from institutional support: schools provide resources like a meeting place, adviser, and easily accessible outreach to other students.
  - You have limited time: running a club requires less time commitment than a full nonprofit organization.
- Hosting a one-time fundraiser
  - You have a specific, short-term goal (e.g., disaster relief or medical bills).
  - You don't need ongoing infrastructure (e.g., your cause doesn't need running programs or continuous support).
  - You have an existing organization you can support.
  - You cannot commit to a long-term or large-scale project.

- Organizing a protest
    - You need immediate, widespread attention: protests can draw urgency around specific issues like the murder of George Floyd or anti-ICE protests against immigrant raids.
    - Your issue can generate public visibility and mass mobilization: if you have a community supporting your cause, seeing and feeling the movement can create immense change.
- Lobbying
    - You need policy change: if a specific law, regulation, or government policy is at the root of the issue, this form of social action is best.
    - You have strong research and advocacy skills, or politicians in your network: drawing up compelling evidence, writing policy papers, and meeting with legislators is key to this role. If you're interested in political science, public policy, international relations, government, history, or the legal field, this may be a better option for you!
- Creating an app
    - Technology can tackle the problem: think of automating a process, tracking data, or making information more accessible as the solution to your target problem of interest.
    - You have or can acquire technical skills.
- Starting a podcast or social media channel
    - You want to raise awareness or educate people about the problem.
    - You like talking and being in front of a camera.
    - You hope to build a community and regularly engage members.
- Writing a book, blog, or literary piece (this very book is an example!)
    - You have a unique perspective, personal story, or expertise to share, and there is a market for it.

- Your end goal is to leave people more educated on a topic.
- You're prepared for a long writing, publishing, and marketing journey.

While this list is not meant to deter you from starting an organization, it is extremely important that you understand what it takes to start and lead a successful nonprofit in order to be ready to embark on this journey. Sometimes, that means spending months—or even years—planning and assessing. For example, Lea Nepomuceno, the founder of Beauty Beyond Bars, began conducting interviews with formerly incarcerated individuals at the age of thirteen as part of a social-impact-oriented summer program. This experience inspired her to start a journalism project focused on interviewing formerly incarcerated people across the United States to break the negative stigma and improve the criminal justice system through stories. For four years, Lea sat down and conversed with members of the incarcerated community.

In these interviews, Lea began realizing a common problem that emerged: a lack of hygienic products. Folks she interviewed discussed bathroom fights over toilet paper and bartering systems for shampoo, items Lea thought of as essentials. She was spurred to start a nonprofit, Beauty Beyond Bars, to address this crisis.

Lea's nonprofit journey is a prime example of an individual who transformed a personal interaction into a meaningful organization. She also took the time, four years, to fully understand the population Beauty Beyond Bars was intended to support by talking one-on-one with incarcerated individuals and listening to their stories. It's clear that Lea noticed an unaddressed problem and decided to utilize her talents to make a change. These characteristics are shared among the strongest young nonprofit leaders.

You should only start a nonprofit if

- You have new ideas on how to address a problem.
- You have a unique set of skills.

- ▸ You like leading a team or creating your own solutions.

- ▸ You want to make a tangible impact.

- ▸ You have resources (people, funding, technology, etc.) to support your endeavor.

- ▸ You have intentions to address this problem over a long span of time.

- ▸ You would be willing to give up movie nights and hours of TikTok scrolling per day to solve this problem (aka you'd be willing to devote *time* and *energy* to this endeavor and make sacrifices).

In other words: Do you see a gap that you *and only you* can help fill? It's that founder-market fit!

Identifying a Problem

It was 3:07 a.m.

In the darkness of my bedroom, I lay frozen as silent sobs racked my body. Tears streamed down my face, wetting my T-shirt.

Grief is a funny thing.

In the summer of 2019, I lost both my grandfather and my former elementary school teacher to cancer. Ms. Michelle (name changed for privacy reasons) took care of me every day after school while my mother worked late; she served as my closest confidant, and I visited her throughout middle school. My grandfather, a teacher himself, shaped me into who I am today during each summer visit and FaceTime call. When both Ms. Michelle and my grandfather succumbed to cancer in quick succession, grief, fear, and anger erupted within me. I fell into a dark place; I had never processed loss of this kind before.

My light at the end of the tunnel came when my family reminded me of who they were: two people who lived to give back. While I could not change what had happened, I was in control of my response to the situation. I wanted to honor my two loved ones while carrying on their legacy of putting their students first. I was going to put kids with cancer first (do you see where our name, Cancer Kids First, came from now?).

When my grandfather was first diagnosed, I started selling my artwork—bookmarks, binder covers, and more—to raise money for his treatment. After he passed, the funds went to childhood cancer research. But seeing him endure chemotherapy in China and learning more about the gaps in care for young patients made me realize that fundraising alone wasn't enough. I wanted to do more. Losing Ms. Michelle only reinforced that—it was the final push that made me build something lasting.

And so, I decided to start a nonprofit organization. I didn't know how I would do it yet, but at that moment, I promised myself, my grandfather, and Ms. Michelle that it would be *the* youth-led nonprofit that patients could turn to in times of distress.

It all happened very spur of the moment. That night, I sat on my bedroom floor, surrounded by five blank sheets of paper—each one labeled for team structure, our mission, logo ideas, one-year goals, and potential partners.

With my glasses on and the screen set to the lowest brightness level in an effort not to catch my parents' notice, I opened Google and furiously began researching. I was always a perfectionist and poured 110 percent into every project I took on, so I was going to learn everything I could about starting a successful nonprofit.

That night, I read a total of eighty-seven articles. As I assembled the bits and pieces of what I saw as the next steps, I jotted down notes and generated brain maps on my five blank sheets.

For the next week, I planned and planned CKF. Sometimes, when an idea struck in the middle of the night, I would get up, reach for the sticky notepad and the pencil next to my pillow, and jot down my thoughts so I would not forget them. (Fun fact: this is still how I come up with new leadership positions like community relations director.)

I would wake up to twenty Post-it notes scattered around my room in the morning. My middle-of-the-night writing was never legible, but I soon had ideas for every aspect of my nonprofit, from the website layout to the systematic way we would onboard volunteers.

Hopefully, the start of your journey is a little easier than this. Some of you may have a strong desire to address a specific problem—maybe your brother has autism, so you want to raise awareness for students with disabilities. Or, maybe you have gone through a life-changing hospital experience and want to give back to other children dealing with life-threatening illnesses. Even if you don't have that specific problem you want to solve right now, that's OK. There are plenty of places to look for inspiration.

The most important thing is to build your nonprofit around something you *truly care about*. Don't choose an issue just to follow a trend. Turn to your surroundings, background, and community for ideas. Perhaps it's an issue you, your friends, your classmates, and your family have faced. Maybe it's an issue on the national news or the "hot topic" in your school's cafeteria that you just can't stop thinking about. Passion is what sustains you through late nights, rejection emails, and burnout. When the work gets tough, it's your personal connection to the cause that will keep you going.

Natalie Guo, an investor at Thrive Capital and the founder of the nonprofit Off Their Plate, once told me that everyone has a passion—a topic that excites you *so much* you could spend every free minute thinking, writing, researching every corner of the web to learn everything about that topic. You feel a spark every time you work on the project.

For me, that topic was childhood cancer. Every minute of every hour was spent thinking about CKF. What could be improved? How could we grow it? I couldn't shut that voice off in my head, and I didn't want to.

Shut this book, and close your eyes. What topic ignites that sensation for you?

As you consider what ignites your passion, make sure your topic is not too specific or too general. You don't want to pick something that would not gather supporters (donors, volunteers, or partners) or an issue that won't be pertinent for years to come. For example, many COVID-19 youth-led nonprofits have now transitioned to helping food banks or hospitals generally rather than COVID-specific patients. For many of these organizations, starting a one-time or smaller-scale service project may have been a more suitable option than going through all the steps of founding a nonprofit. Thinking about the long term will prove vital for sustainable success. In a few chapters, we'll go through more specific exercises to refine your organization's mission statement to achieve this.

Additionally, since there are already millions of nonprofits out there, it is important for founders to engage in community mapping: see what work is already out there and if there are projects you can collaborate with other young people on, rather than duplicating their efforts.

CHECKLIST FOR THE IDENTIFIED PROBLEM

- ☐ I care about this because it relates to something in my personal life (a problem that's affected me, my loved ones, or my community).

- ☐ I could explain this problem to someone who knows nothing about it.

- ☐ I have opinions about this problem and ideas for solutions that don't currently exist.

- ☐ I see this problem staying relevant for years to come.

- ☐ I know this problem impacts individuals, groups, places, or animals.

If you meet all five, your "identified problem" is in good shape!

Here are some samples to help you self-evaluate your problem statement to ensure it is in the best shape to launch a nonprofit.

Identified problem: I did a research project on the opioid epidemic and want to raise awareness about it.

Why it needs work: This statement lacks a personal or lived connection—a research project suggests recent exposure, not deep-rooted experience. It's also vague ("raise awareness" about what exactly?) and doesn't acknowledge the many organizations already addressing the issue.

Identified problem: I recently earned my barber's license after completing 1,500-plus hours of training. During that time, I cut the hair of over 200 individuals—many of whom were homeless, people of color, or living in poverty. I heard stories of struggle, shame, and a lack of access to grooming. These services are not a luxury—they shape confidence, identity, and dignity.

Why it works: This problem is rooted in lived experience, centers a specific underserved population, and highlights a clear gap. It's personal, tangible, and tied to an ongoing need.

Types of 501(c)(3) Nonprofits

Once you've identified the problem you want to solve, the next step is choosing what kind of nonprofit to build. Nonprofits generally fall into four categories:

1. SERVICE-BASED OR DIRECT DONATION NONPROFITS: These organizations provide direct aid or services—think Doctors Without Borders offering medical care in conflict zones, or groups donating hygiene products to shelters. Whether it's distributing goods or offering performances in nursing homes, this model meets immediate needs.

2. AWARENESS OR ADVOCACY NONPROFITS WITH A LEGISLATIVE LENS: The importance of awareness can fall through the cracks at times. Many people neglect, or even forget, the power of knowledge. And, for many critical issues, understanding the problem at its core is vital for appropriate problem-solving. These nonprofits focus on educating the public and influencing policy. Groups like the National Alliance on Mental Illness and the World Wildlife Fund use their knowledge to fight stigma, shift narratives, and advocate for legislation. Their power lies in mobilizing communities and driving systemic change through awareness and policy reform.

3. FUNDRAISING AND GRANTMAKING NONPROFITS: Organizations in this category raise and distribute funds to support causes, research, or other nonprofits. For example, the Leukemia & Lymphoma Society funds cancer research, while the Ford Foundation supports social justice initiatives through grants.

4. SOCIAL CHANGE ADVOCACY NONPROFITS: Often overlooked, these nonprofits lead transformation by reshaping social norms and public discourse.

Take the feminist movement, for example—many nonprofits focus on shifting cultural attitudes through public speak-outs, art, viral campaigns, or bystander trainings rather than legislation or services. Similarly, climate justice groups may use boycotts or demonstrations to challenge consumer behavior and pressure corporations for accountability.

These forms of advocacy are powerful precisely because they target the social fabric in which harmful norms are embedded. Sriram Bhimaraju—a nineteen-year-old founder of Seas Brighter Foundation—exemplifies just how advocacy can play a central role in cultural change ecosystems. Seeking to educate international youth on climate awareness, Sriram hosted a book launch event for his environmental awareness book. One third grader, inspired by his event, went on to organize her own Earth Day campaign. Other kids he spoke to reported that they created their own climate art to display in their town centers and began refusing to use plastic bags when grocery shopping.

Once Sriram spread that little piece of information about ongoing harms to the environment, he didn't have to do anything else but watch as that knowledge empowered someone else to lead change. His story underscores a key truth: as a nonprofit leader, your impact isn't limited to what *you* do directly—it often comes through the people you empower. Use your organization to spread important messages, and let others bring change into their own circles.

Choosing the right type of nonprofit matters. Your mission, community, and desired partnerships should all inform your model. If your cause is mental health, for instance, awareness and advocacy may be more effective than direct services. Similarly, direct service groups may partner with local hospitals, while advocacy groups align more with media and government entities.

Many nonprofits combine elements: advocacy/awareness and direct service tend to be a popular combination because many issues require both a "Band-aid" solution (the donation of items or services) and a long-term solution (new policy or legislation or a shift in conversation). Think about environmental nonprofits, for instance. Effective conservation efforts need both timely reforestation projects and legislation to drive change over the next decades.

You don't need to stress about mapping out exactly which of these methods you want to use. Aspects of them can be added on throughout the years. Maybe you start with direct service but supplement it with a mentorship program once your team is large enough, or once you gain a deeper understanding of the underlying inequities and injustices like in the case of Beauty Beyond Bars. Running an organization is about adapting to internal and external changes!

2

The Power of YOUth: Leveraging Your Age

WHEN WE ARE YOUNG, we often find ourselves longing for the next stage of life—waiting to turn eighteen or twenty-one, get married, or become parents. We spend so much time looking ahead, believing that those older than we are must be "cooler" or "more fun." Think about it—how many times did you imagine how exciting high school would be while you were in middle school, only to get there and start dreaming about college life?

Society places a strong emphasis on age as a measure of credibility, equating it with experience and wisdom. So, it's natural that many of you who are considering starting a nonprofit would have the doubt "Why would anyone take me seriously?"

But when it comes to driving social change, your age is not a limitation—it's an asset. The most influential movements in history have been fueled by young people who dared to challenge norms, think differently, and take action.

This chapter explores how you can embrace and leverage YOUth as a strength so you're prepared with the right mindset and attitude before getting into the nitty gritty of it all.

Why YOUth?

Your biggest question may be why you should start a nonprofit *now*. Why not wait until you're older? Are there unique advantages to being a young founder?

The answer is a compelling *yes*. In the previous chapter, I spent a lot of time setting the stage for how young people should only start a nonprofit if they've truly thought it through—identifying a real, overlooked problem they're passionate about solving and making sure they have the commitment and mindset to lead. When those pieces are in place, being a youth leader becomes a powerful advantage.

PEER-TO-PEER POWER: Youth-led organizations are built by and for young people, which creates immediate relatability and trust. We know what drives young people—because we are them—so we can capitalize on that knowledge to market our organizations well. In other words, youth leaders are well positioned to rapidly mobilize communities.

Motivations can be separated into extrinsic motivations, stemming from external sources, such as rewards, praise, or punishment, and intrinsic motivations driven by personal enjoyment, interest, and satisfaction in the activity itself.[1] Extrinsically, young people are often motivated by opportunities that help them grow and build their future—like earning service hours, strengthening their résumés, or receiving letters of recommendation. Because community service and skill building are such common focuses during our teenage and college years, we're in a unique position to attract other youth volunteers by highlighting these benefits. On an intrinsic level, young people are naturally drawn to meaningful stories and social issues.

When youth leaders create the messaging, tone, and strategy—especially on platforms like TikTok, Instagram, and Discord—it feels more authentic and relatable to other young people, making it easier to inspire action and build community.

Beyond online outreach, young people have built-in social networks they can easily tap into for team members, volunteers, and supporters. From school clubs and sports teams to summer programs and classmates, youth leaders have access to concentrated, close-knit communities that make launching a nonprofit more manageable. In contrast, adults often find it harder to mobilize their in-person networks, which tend to be more spread out and less connected.

Finally, young leaders are often more nimble, responsive, and able to mobilize peers quickly around a cause using DMs, texts, and group chats.

FRESH AND UNFILTERED: Adults may blame it on social media, but one thing's for sure: young people are unafraid to question authority or break the mold—whether that means starting a nonprofit in high school or organizing protests at schools. This boldness helps push the boundaries of what's possible, and it's why young people are often at the head of movements in climate action, racial justice, mental health, and education reform.

Because young people will inherit the future, we have more at stake—we have "skin in the game." This personal investment gives us a strong reason to care deeply about the world's problems. When we communicate that urgency to funders and partners, it strengthens our case for why our work matters.

At the same time, growing up with social media and now AI has shaped how we see the world. It naturally makes us question traditional methods and ask, "Can this be done better?" That fresh perspective is valuable, whether it leads to starting a new nonprofit or helping existing ones evolve and stay relevant in a changing world.

Last but not least, many youth organizations are formed out of personal experiences—grief, injustice, identity—not revolving around careers. This emotional connection leads to deep commitment and the willingness to challenge "how things have always been done."

DIGITAL-NATIVE LEADERSHIP: Gen Z and beyond know technology like no other. Youth leaders are naturals at online organizing, social media campaigns, and digital storytelling. This makes it easier to go viral not through money, but through creativity and message resonance. Virality can then be translated into partnerships, volunteers, and donors.

Aside from growth, being fluent in technology allows young leaders to streamline key organizational processes. For example, we can quickly identify the best communication tools for team messaging, select efficient project management platforms, automate routine tasks, and use data tools to track impact and make informed decisions. This tech-savviness helps nonprofits run more smoothly and adapt quickly—especially in a rapidly changing digital landscape.

Proving Age Is Just a Number

Despite the many advantages of being a youth leader, adults often underestimate the power of YOUth. Age-based doubt is common, but establishing credibility is crucial—and possible—through both personal authenticity and measurable impact.

Sreenidi Bala, founder of Code for All Minds (CFAM), used her personal story to gain trust. CFAM is a first-of-its-kind computer science education program for neurodivergent students. Growing up, Sreenidi's best friend had autism, so Sreenidi often helped in her school's special learning classroom. She realized that despite the students' talents and verbal abilities, all of them were being prepared for careers in labor-intensive industries; there were no STEM opportunities available. Thus, during the pandemic, Sreenidi filmed tutorial videos that built up the STEM and computer efficiency skills of neurodivergent students. After noticing the impact of these videos, she established an elective class at her high school that eventually became the blueprint for CFAM.

To authentically connect with adults and bring CFAM to life, Sreenidi shared her founding story. By immediately breaking the ice through personal impetus, Sreenidi helped adults focus on her mission, not her age. Particularly, Sreenidi focused on how she started her work in the classroom simply to help her friends, which then led to the success she saw in her own school's elective class, and the impact she hoped to generate with further support.

Others, like Shrusti Amula, a sophomore at Georgetown University, found success using a data-driven approach. Shrusti's 501(c)(3) nonprofit, Rise N Shine, is dedicated to reducing food waste through composting and food-recovery programs. She highlighted facts—such as food waste being the third-largest cause of climate change—to capture attention and support.

Finally, reflecting on the three advantages of being young mentioned earlier, you can use your age as a strength to rally support from your school, clubs, or peers. Once you've built community, leverage that support system—those numbers behind you—to open doors with adults. Mentors and advisers can then help you turn those connections into concrete opportunities. This allows you to confidently say, "I'm a high schooler trying to . . . ," as a unique selling point—not a drawback. And when you're unsure or need extra credibility, don't hesitate to lean on adult allies for follow-through and guidance.

Pitch Perfect

As a young person, there's no doubt that commanding a room and getting adults to agree to work with you is difficult. That's why the art of the elevator pitch can take you far, whether it's a quick spiel over the phone or an in-person meeting. The term "elevator pitch" comes from the idea of pitching a new project or initiative to someone in the average time of a quick elevator ride: thirty to sixty seconds.[2] As young leaders, we are even more reliant on storytelling, data, and preparation to help us gain respect.

How I usually structure elevator pitches is as follows (note: you can apply this same format to elevator pitches for jobs, college admissions, awards, and more):

1. YOUR PAST: Why did you start your nonprofit? Why is the issue important? How have your childhood, family experiences, previous extracurriculars, values, etc. influenced your nonprofit journey?

2. YOUR PRESENT: What are your nonprofit's current stats? Biggest achievements? Recent projects that you're excited about? What sets you apart from others?

3. YOUR FUTURE: How do you plan to take your organization to the next level? How can XYZ (whoever you're pitching to) align with your goals? How can you and your nonprofit uniquely contribute to XYZ based on your past experiences and present work?

The goal is to structure your nonprofit story into three time blocks, making it digestible, organized, and easy to follow. Adults are drawn to passion and energy—two qualities that young people uniquely possess. Growing up in a different generation brings new experiences and perspectives, which can be powerfully conveyed through storytelling. Instead of just telling your story, *show* it by describing emotions, time, place, and other key details. Engage adults with your journey, then reinforce your impact with a few concrete numbers (e.g., "We now have fifteen schools on board to provide school supplies across three counties in California!" rather than "We help unprivileged students") to establish credibility.

Breaking down the elevator pitch structure further, most adults underestimate the power of YOUth; they don't see us as capable of creating and leading long-lasting, impactful initiatives, so use that element of surprise to capture adults' attention. For the first time block, your Past, mention the age at which you started your organization and how far you've come since its founding. For example, Diana Chao, the founder of Letters to Strangers, may say, "I grew up with bipolar disorder and c-PTSD and didn't believe I deserved the air I breathed. After surviving both suicide loss and attempt, I found healing from an unexpected source: writing. So as a sophomore in high school, I founded Letters to Strangers, which has since grown into the largest global youth mental health organization. We've impacted 500,000 people worldwide."

For the second time block, your Present, mention ways your organization is unique. Young people bring new ideas and digital fluency that older generations may not have. Position yourself as innovative. For example, let's say you are pitching a partnership proposal to a well-established nonprofit in your field that is composed of professionals. You could mention how while traditional fundraising (which they most likely engage in) relies on in-person campaigning, utilizing TikTok and Instagram Reels has driven thousands of dollars in donations from across the world. You can also mention how being entirely youth run means there's an untapped market potential that traditional nonprofits may not have access to: Gen Alpha (or your generation at the time of reading this book).

For the last time block, your Future, ensure you think about what you need and how you can help the other party. Be bold in your ask. Instead of a general "Would you consider supporting us?" you can ask, "With your support of a $1,000 grant, we can impact 500 more students."

Finally, for all three time blocks, ensure you tap into that infectious energy and optimism young leaders possess. Speak with conviction, letting your passion show. People invest in passion just as much as they do in ideas. If you're struggling to find confidence in your pitching—whether it's because of nerves or something else—I recommend adopting quick and easy strategies to boost your self-confidence. I'll mention pep talks throughout this book, but another quick and easy strategy you can use before a pitch or meeting is power posing. A power pose is simply an open, expansive stance. Some common ones are "the victory pose" (raise your hands or fists above your head in a V shape) or "the Wonder Woman" (stand up straight, chin up, and place your hands on your hips or sides). As stupid as it may look, it's scientifically proven that power posing increases testosterone levels, a hormone associated with dominance and confidence, while simultaneously decreasing levels of cortisol, a stress-related hormone.[3]

Rehearse your elevator pitch over and over again so that you memorize the basic framework but can still improvise small details. You don't want it to sound like a script, but you want to make sure you hit all the key points you want to mention! Practice the pitch in front of others to get used to sharing it with an audience, and seek feedback to refine your points. As a general rule of thumb, try to keep your elevator pitch around thirty seconds to a minute and a half. Depending on the circumstances, you could expand it to two minutes. I know that seems like an absurdly short amount of time to convey your entire nonprofit story, but remember that the human attention span is short!

Stepping into *Your* Identity—*and Owning It*

To continue building your leadership mindset, it's important to understand the difference between managers and leaders. While managers simply command a group of people, leaders nurture themselves and those around them. While managers simply assign tasks, leaders inspire, motivate, and support. Obviously, the latter is better for developing a strong team and organization that achieves its objectives. Learning to become a great leader can also positively affect other aspects of your life as you learn to communicate, encourage others, and foster a fulfilling environment. While some people may seem "born to lead," I believe leadership is a skill you build through experience.

With the rise of social media and digital platforms such as LinkedIn, glorifying our lives—and in turn, our achievements—has become more common. But those platforms can sometimes set the wrong expectations for success and for what leadership actually looks like. Being a leader isn't just about the title of "CEO" or the fancy accolades you may receive in recognition of your work. You're being a leader when you simply sit down at the breakfast table and talk to your family about a difficult topic; everyone's a leader in their own space.

People always said I was a natural leader—organizing trips, managing group projects, and taking charge in clubs from a young age. But that didn't mean I was ready to run a nonprofit. When I launched Cancer Kids First as a freshman, I was shy around adults and terrified of rejection. After receiving sixty-plus partnership rejections, I started downplaying CKF, framing it as just a "small project." I was scared people wouldn't take me seriously, so I preemptively belittled myself and the work I was doing.

But, this attitude was only limiting myself and CKF's future. You do not need to be a "natural-born leader" to be a good nonprofit CEO, but you do have to realize two things:

1. HUMANS ARE INCREDIBLY SELF-ABSORBED: More often than not, others are more worried about themselves than about paying attention to you and your mistakes. So, if you mess up or fail and people are there to witness it, they'll forget about it soon enough. And as Barack Obama said, "You can't let your failures define you—you have to let your failures teach you." Failure builds resilience and resilience builds you into a better person.

2. IF YOU DON'T BELIEVE IN YOURSELF, NO ONE ELSE WILL: Confidence is contagious. "Fake it 'til you make it" works because humans cling to each other (as a society, we unfortunately really care about what others think) and generally adopt the herd mentality—the tendency for people to think and act like the group. If you act like you believe in yourself, others will too.

No matter where you are in your leadership journey, you should adopt tactics to build your confidence—or at least methods to fake it.

You need to persuade yourself and others that you are a motherf*cking *boss*. (If you've seen the TikTok trends, it's like adopting the mindset that you're the main character . . . because you are, and this is *your* story.)

Here are some of my favorite ways to start cultivating that confidence to drive your leadership forward:

FACING YOUR FEARS, CHASING YOUR DREAMS, AND ACCOMPLISHING YOUR GOALS: Comparing my college freshman self to my high school freshman self is astounding. In a mere four years, I transformed into someone who was confident (in who I was and as a leader), passionate, and ambitious because I accomplished goals and milestones I had set for myself. Facing your fears and achieving goals, even mini ones like waking up early every morning, will make you proud of yourself. Confidence comes with that because you get to look back and say, "*Damn*, I did that." So, challenge yourself every day—or every week or every month—to do something that scares you but that you've always wanted to do. Or, write out a list of goals (they can be personal, professional, or academic) and "deadlines" to achieve them.

POSITIVE AFFIRMATIONS: Sometimes, all it takes is a little pick-me-up pep talk to get you going. Before meetings or large events, I often go in front of a mirror and give myself a pep talk, as stupid as it sounds. I remind myself of everything I have already accomplished and state the strengths I know I possess. I started doing this after my first meeting with a room full of adult men. (I was sweating buckets . . . and they were all in suits!! Talk about nerve-racking for a fifteen-year-old.) It gave me enough confidence to enter the meeting room and pitch CKF without stuttering.

POSITIVE ATTRACTS POSITIVE: You need positive people in your life. A support network will help chase away those negative thoughts and feelings that cloud your mind. I sometimes like to imagine a positive aura emitting from me, one that glows brighter when I meet other positive individuals. I strongly believe that energy matters!

SELF-LOVE: Honestly, I think confidence boils down to self-love. Now, there's a difference between being cocky or egotistical and knowing your worth. I think it's so important to love yourself, especially to build confidence, because you need to be proud of and happy about yourself. In fact, you deserve to. This can look different for each person, but it can range from working out and eating healthy to dressing well so that you feel and look your best.

BOOKS, PODCASTS, AND OTHER MEDIA: I read countless leadership books throughout my nonprofit journey. From *Springboard: Launching Your Personal Search for Success* by G. Richard Shell to *Grit: The Power of Passion and Perseverance* by Angela Duckworth, I soaked up the advice of other leaders and changemakers. I also listened to podcasts like *The Happiness Lab* with Dr. Laurie Santos and *Anything Goes* by Emma Chamberlain to shape my mindset. Even movies like *The Intern* (so good, especially for female CEOs!!) gave me boosts of motivation and knowledge to change the negative ways I thought about situations.

Embracing your identity as a leader is the first step toward becoming a successful CEO. Your confidence and positive energy will radiate outward to the rest of your team and will show up in your work and conversations. You'll start attracting more supporters and partners because people can *see* and *feel* when someone is confident and happy. Let yourself *shine*.

I truly owe it to CKF for building my confidence, especially as a woman of color. Previously, I've felt pressure to make myself more palatable for others by embracing certain mannerisms and rejecting others. But, CKF taught me the importance of being authentic. It transformed the way I think of myself, which then changed how I interacted with others. I became more vocal about CKF and the other projects I was passionate about. I started seeking more opportunities to elevate my brand, and that is the reason why I've been able to share my story at so many conferences and on podcasts, news sites, and social media. Comments I get that try to diminish me or my work hardly affect me. I'm no longer scared to pursue the goals that I want to, and that feeling is unlike any other because it's *freeing*.

If you need a bit more of a boost, take a note from Sophia Kianni, a twenty-four-year-old Iranian American social entrepreneur and climate activist as well as the founder of Climate Cardinals. Sophia keeps both a list on her Notes app and a handwritten notecard where she writes small wins and successes that she can look back on and reference.

The digital and physical notes give her something direct to examine in moments of self-doubt. Adopting a method like this can give you a much-needed boost of confidence before a daunting presentation or just serve as a small pick-me-up when you're stressed.

3

Planning, Prepping, and Prototyping

NOW YOU'RE READY to get into the weeds of starting a nonprofit. You've picked your problem and now understand how you can leverage your age to address that problem. To shape your solution into a tangible plan, you need to start thinking about your name, logo, mission statement, and service programs.

Name and Logo

Your organization's name and logo play a critical role in the branding of your nonprofit. It becomes what everyone associates with you and your work, so be mindful when picking out names and logos.

Beauty Beyond Bars has an insightful name origin story. Lea was originally experimenting with the name Beauty Behind Bars, since the triple-B acronym made the shortened nonprofit name fun and memorable while effectively communicating what they do as an organization: bring beauty behind bars. But, Lea wanted a name that made it clear her organization was committed to building a world where everyone is empowered to look good, feel good, and do good from behind bars and beyond prison. Simply adjusting "Behind" to "Beyond" created a whole new meaning for their work, encompassing everything the organization does outside of donating beauty and hygiene products, such as their legislative campaigns. Their new and improved name shapes their motto, "We bring beauty behind bars and the conversation *beyond*." As we delve into what a mission statement is and its importance, think about how you can connect your organization name to your mission statement.

The following are some tips to keep in mind when creating a name. Alternative suggestions include looking at what other nonprofits or companies in your nonprofit sector are calling their organizations, as well as utilizing random name generators for inspiration. Generative AI, like ChatGPT, can also be great at sparking ideas, or consider reaching out to your friends, family, and community!

CHECKLIST FOR *THE* NAME

- ☐ It aligns with your mission statement and target service group (e.g., if it's a nonprofit serving kids, you don't want the name to contain challenging words).

- ☐ It's easy to remember and fairly simple. (Some name styles are descriptive, like Boys & Girls Clubs of America and Feeding America, while others are acronyms like UNICEF and PETA.)

- ☐ It'll perform well in search engine optimization strategies (aka will your organization be googleable? Memorable on social media platforms?).

- ☐ It's unique. (Is the name, website domain, or social media username already taken?)

- ☐ It appeals to diverse audiences. (Ask teachers, friends, and even strangers to provide their insights because the broader your initial testing pool is, the more likely your nonprofit's name will resonate with your future audience too!)

Similar to the process of creating a name, you can also look at logo generators or similar nonprofits for design ideas. Looking through Canva sample logos can give you inspiration, as can the logos of the companies you find memorable (Starbucks, Apple, and Nike). Take the time to search through designs and write out what you like about them.

The Paani Project, a 501(c)(3) nonprofit that was first envisioned by Sonny Khan and his friends at the University of Michigan to support sanitation and care in Pakistan, has an eye-catching and representative logo (see figure 1). In fact, Sonny credits the logo with getting people excited about the organization. The Paani Project logo takes the word "water" in Urdu, the official language of Pakistan, and shapes it into a water droplet. Not only is this logo innovative and memorable, but it also directly conveys the nonprofit's mission of constructing water systems with treatment and containment solutions to improve sanitation in Pakistan. Naturally, their logo is colored blue to align with the theme of water.

Are there colors, symbols, or graphics that you associate with your nonprofit and cause? Try those out for your first logo!

When creating my first logo, I drew out some sample designs and asked my friends, family, and leadership team to vote. I then asked a friend who is a digital artist to transfer the piece of art to a digital image. Notice how I never paid for someone to create a design; as a youth founder, it's important to utilize the resources around you to save costs!

FIGURE 1: Paani Project logo. *Source: Paani Project. Used with permission.*

CHECKLIST FOR *THE* LOGO

☐   It aligns with your mission statement and target service group. (Think: Are there particular colors or graphics associated with your cause? For instance, pink is tied with breast cancer.)

☐   You researched color psychology and selected colors that fit your organization. (Colors psychologically evoke different emotions; read up on what colors may signal and which colors mesh well together!)

☐   It's timeless.

☐   It looks good big or small and on various platforms (digitally, in print, displayed across a giant poster, etc.).

☐   It matches your brand personality. (Do you want something electric and modern or fun and playful?)

☐   It stands out from similar nonprofits.

☐   It represents keywords that reflect your cause (e.g., community, love, or empowerment).

Mission Statement and Service Programs

A solid mission statement can make or break your nonprofit. It not only shapes the work and services you provide, but it also guides you and your employees, volunteers, partners, investors, and supporters in achieving your organization's goals. Furthermore, it defines your target audience and communicates your core values.

While there aren't strict laws mandating a perfect mission statement, the Internal Revenue Service requires all 501(c)(3) organizations to have an "exempt purpose" that reflects their mission. If your statement is vague or disconnected from your work, you risk losing your tax-exempt status. At a state level, you also must declare a charitable purpose in your articles of incorporation.

Your mission statement should stem from your identified problem and answer four powerful questions:

1. What do we do?

2. How are we doing it?

3. Whom are we helping?

4. What value are we creating?

The best mission statements are concise but specific. Let's look at a few examples:

Too specific: At the Yunnan Turtle Project, we save Yunnan box turtles by signing government petitions and making awareness posters.

Improved: The Yunnan Turtle Project is dedicated to protecting the endangered Yunnan box turtle through advocacy, education, and community-driven conservation efforts.

Too general: The Latin American Association helps Latin American students with schooling.

Improved: The Latin American Association empowers Latin American students through academic support, mentorship, and cultural enrichment programs that foster higher education and career success.

See the difference between the two? Make sure your organization's mission statement is—as Goldilocks put it—just right.

Take Feeding America, one of the world's biggest nonprofits. Their mission statement is to "help people get the food and resources they need to thrive. Everything we do focuses on getting nutritious food to communities—from sourcing food donations to advocating for policies that end hunger."[1] From this statement, you can clearly tell *what* they're doing and *how* they're doing it, and understand *who* they're targeting with their services. Or the American Red Cross: "To prevent and alleviate human suffering in the face of emergencies by mobilizing the power of volunteers and the generosity of donors."[2] Once again, it's specific enough to understand the field they're serving and how, but it also leaves enough room for interpretation to allow for the expansion of service programs and partnerships.

I'll be honest—my own organization didn't get it right the first time. Cancer Kids First's original mission (which we officially wrote to the IRS on our first government form) was "To donate toys and books to pediatric cancer hospitals and patients across the U.S."

I still cringe when I look back at it—at the time, I did not think about the future plans of our organization. This mission statement was limiting us to the services we could provide (only toys and books) and the scope of impact we could create (only in the United States). Needless to say, we eventually changed it to our current mission statement, which describes how we "strive to normalize the hospital environment and build a supportive community for kids with cancer."[3] This gives us the flexibility to implement a variety of service programs to bring hospital resources, arts and crafts, interactive events, and more to patients internationally. The latter half of the mission statement also highlights one of our nonprofit's unique factors: our large and diverse youth team whose goal is to build bonds with patients.

The greatest nonprofit mission statements also come from taking the time and energy to research the cause you are addressing. Conducting a needs assessment, interview, focus group, or other form of feedback can give you a clear picture of the needs facing your target community. Gather insights from your family, friends, and mentors to craft a succinct message that represents the vision you have for your nonprofit. Once your mission is clear, it will inform the design of your service programs. And here's the exciting part: service programs give life to your mission. They're the *how* behind your *why*.

When it comes to service programs, you have a lot of creative freedom! Go back to the categories of nonprofits I listed in the previous chapter; if your organization is advocacy-centric, lobbying or pushing for social change may not fit squarely in a service program. You may need to determine your needs for service programs accordingly.

Before launching a program, assess the real needs of your target community. This could be emailing your target service group or experts in the field of your choice. If you're starting a literacy nonprofit, talk to teachers and librarians. If your mission centers on disability access, reach out to special education professionals, students, and parents. Your goal is to understand the root challenges your community faces—and what's already being done to solve them.

Look around your space. What are other nonprofits doing well? What gaps remain? You don't want to duplicate services unless you can offer something uniquely valuable.

Also, be sure your programs align with your mission. If you say your goal is to conserve the environment by mobilizing youth, your services should reflect that—tree planting, educational workshops, or sustainable-product drives—not just general awareness campaigns. Ensuring your service programs match your mission statement will keep volunteers and other stakeholders engaged and committed.

The best nonprofits combine research with creativity. Letters to Strangers, the largest global youth-for-youth mental health nonprofit, has created a wide range of impacts that have garnered recognition from Selena Gomez and the Rare Beauty fund, as well as from Lady Gaga and the Born This Way Foundation. Their programs fall into three clear paths:

1. **Letter writing**: Anonymous peer support through heartfelt letters

2. **Peer education**: Mental health workshops and training for schools

3. **Policy-based advocacy**: Systemic change via task forces and partnerships with school administrators

Each pathway aligns directly with their mission and creates a unique layer of impact.

Another avenue to look at when creating service programs is available resources. Think about the number of committed volunteers, your team's skill sets, funding, and available materials. Planning service programs that reach too far beyond the resources available can be detrimental.

By understanding the needs of your community and doing adequate back-end work before you get started, you can better create an impactful organization that is more likely to benefit your target audience and secure partnerships and funding.

Once you come up with a few ideas for your service programs, get ready to launch! You can hold a few pilot events and evaluate their impact before officially launching them as a part of your organization. Think low-cost and high-impact events like donation drives, workshops, or virtual events. As a student, you may want to hold initial events at your school or local businesses, libraries, or community spaces to test the waters. For instance, great initial events include a trash clean-up day for an environmental nonprofit or a workshop with an author for an educational literacy nonprofit.

I also want to note that while putting thought into your mission statement and service programs is important, they are not set in stone. You can still make changes—and you should even consider making changes, especially to service programs—as time goes on, but it is a multistep process. For an organization's mission statement, you must update organizational documents—particularly your articles of incorporation—and external communications like your website, donor materials, social media, etc. If your new mission shifts your nonprofit's core purpose (e.g., from education to health care), you must also notify the IRS in your Form 990 filing (more on legal forms in the "Toolbox for Changemakers" section) and possibly write a letter to your assigned IRS agent or file Form 8940 for formal approval. Changes to service programs usually just need to be updated in your public materials.

Take Alley-Oop, a youth-led nonprofit that originally tackled a range of projects promoting youth play—from basketball camps to sports video tutorials—during COVID. While impactful, their programming lacked focus. Eventually, under Rishan Patel, a high school senior and Alley-Oop's new CEO, they pivoted to a single, scalable idea: "Lending Lockers" filled with free sports gear for underresourced schools. Today, they've built over 250 lockers serving 200,000-plus students.

The impact that Alley-Oop has had is amazing, but it is their transformation in programming that's even more inspiring. They were able to change their focus to home in on their organization's niche, which ultimately led them to create a deeper impact, since Alley-Oop could pour more time, resources, and energy into a specific creation: Lending Lockers.

What does this tell you as another young nonprofit founder? Don't be afraid to run with your initial idea and programs. Just make sure that you continuously monitor your work and assess whether you need to shift course at any point. Creating and running service programs is often an ongoing, collaborative process. Even after you launch your organization, you may need to add, remove, or adjust your nonprofit's service programs based on trends—the COVID-19 pandemic, for instance, threw everyone for a loop—and changing needs. Keeping flexible will better equip your organization to face unpredictable and uncontrollable challenges like the pandemic.

Financials

While your programs may shift over time, your nonprofit's financial foundation needs to be solid from the beginning. Setting up finances for your nonprofit is a crucial first step in translating your ideas into action. Generally, a nonprofit's finances go hand in hand with its legal forms because many annual legal forms require financial transactions to be included. The "Toolbox for Changemakers" at the back of the book will cover the financial aspects of legal forms, but there is additional financial documentation that I will cover in this section that can ensure transparency within your team and for your donors.

Learning how to create a budget is a skill that will serve you well not only in running your nonprofit but also in your future as you develop independence and step into adult responsibilities.

Have you ever planned an event like a birthday party? Finances are a key consideration to keep in mind to make the event possible. You probably had to think about how much money you had to spend on the birthday party, what you needed to purchase, and how to ensure you had enough money to throw the best birthday party. A financial budget for your nonprofit works the same way.

I suggest starting out with an annual budget recorded in a spreadsheet-like format and planning the budget a few months before the start of the next fiscal (financial) year. Planning financials ahead of time will serve you well throughout the rest of your fiscal year to prevent overspending and keep the organization running.

First, map out your goal(s) for the year: Are you hoping to expand your operations by X percent? Or tackle two new target regions? Depending on this goal, your budgeting should reflect this. To break a budget down into the simplest form, you should look at income (money coming in) and expenses (money going out).

Based on your goal(s) for the year, estimate the expenses you will need for operational costs, program costs, marketing, administration, and more. Always include a contingency fund that can cover costs in case of an emergency. As a baseline, for your organization's first year, plan to spend a couple of thousand dollars. This could look like $1,000 for your first program (kits, campaigns, events, etc.); $600 for nonprofit registration with the state and the IRS; $300 for administrative services (fundraising platforms, websites, Zoom accounts, Canva Pro, etc.); and $200 for contingencies.

Additionally, plan the various income sources for your nonprofit, whether they be from donations, fundraisers, or grants. The fundraising chapter will cover the different avenues in greater depth.

You must involve your board of directors or other leadership team members in creating your nonprofit's annual budget to ensure it aligns with the organization's mission. Budgeting tools like Excel can also ease this process by clearly outlining income, expenses, and totals. Table 1 shows an example budget chart for reference.

TABLE 1: Sample budget and revenue

PROJECTED BUDGET AND REVENUE 2025 CANCER KIDS FIRST, INC.		
INCOME		
Projected Income	**Percentage of Income**	**Estimated Budget**
Fundraising	23%	$7,590.00
Donations Individual Donors	6%	$1,980.00
Donations Corporate Donors	22%	$7,260.00
Grants and Awards	48%	$15,840.00
Other	1%	$330.00
Total Projected Income	**100%**	**$33,000.00**
EXPENSES		
Projected Expenses	**Percentage of Expenses**	**Estimated Budget**
Admin	2%	$640.00
Fundraising	1%	$320.00
Care Packages US Care Packages	32%	$10,240.00
Care Packages International Care Packages	13%	$3,840.00
Donation Items Toys and Books	15%	$5,120.00
International Hospital Resources	36%	$11,600.00
Other	1%	$320.00
Total Projected Expenses	**100%**	**$32,000.00**
FIXED EXPENSES		
Emergency Fund	$100.00	

Source: Cancer Kids First Project Budget and Revenue, 2025. Used with permission.

A core reason for creating a budget is to manage your income and expenses. While tracking income and expenses is essential for all corporations, nonprofits are especially expected to maintain financial transparency. Being a nonprofit doesn't mean you can't run a surplus, nor does it mean you shouldn't mind running a loss.

From a legal standpoint, nonprofits are subject to legal and tax reporting requirements at the end of each fiscal year. IRS Form 990 requires nonprofits to submit accurate documentation of their financial records. Failure to do so could result in the revocation of tax-exempt status or in penalties and fines. These requirements exist for good reason: as a society, we grant nonprofits tax-exempt status because we believe they serve the public good. But with that privilege comes responsibility—and unfortunately, there have been bad actors who have abused that trust. Filing accurate and complete documentation demonstrates integrity, accountability, and a commitment to your mission.

From a donor standpoint, nonprofits that are open about how their funds are collected and used build trust, which encourages further donations. And as entities that primarily run on donations, nonprofits are even more incentivized to uphold financial transparency. Plus, it doesn't hurt to know exactly how your money is coming in and being spent in order to efficiently allocate future resources.

To track expenses precisely, utilize a spreadsheet application like Google Sheets or Microsoft Excel. Classify expenditures into categories like administrative expenses (e.g., website domain or legal form costs), event and fundraising expenses (e.g., decorations or venue reservation costs), and program costs (e.g., goods or services costs). This makes it easier to see where funding is being spent, ensuring your team stays aligned with your mission statement.

You can set up your own system for logging income and expenditure, but I recommend maintaining a regular and timely schedule so you don't have transactions piled up. CKF's chief financial officer, for instance, goes through our bank account statements every week to record the money coming in and going out of our accounts. When she is unsure where money is coming from or going, she reaches out to the appropriate team member to double check. Try to keep receipts or digital documentation, particularly for large purchases, to limit future problems or confusion (or fading memories).

Before the annual tax forms are due, your leadership or financial team should work together to conduct a financial audit. An audit is an objective evaluation of a business's financials to confirm their accuracy and completeness. This is the time to go through your spreadsheet and bank account statements to ensure *all* transactions are noted and make sense before submitting documentation to the government. It can be a little stressful, but this process really sets you up for financial success in your personal and professional life!

Creating a bank account specifically for your 501(c)(3) can make spending and receiving donations easier and tracking your income and expenses more effective. You may want to check out multiple banks in your area to see which banks allow minors to start a business checking or savings account. Sometimes, you may need an adult board member or your registered agent (more on this in the "Toolbox for Changemakers") to cosign with you.

When I first went hunting for a bank that would let a minor open a business account, I had to go through three rejections from banks like Citibank and Chase (to make your process easier, I've included a chart outlining different bank options in the "Toolbox for Changemakers"). Finally, I spoke to a representative at my local Bank of America who kindly explained the banking process to me (who knew there were so many differences between a savings and checking account and a credit and debit card for businesses??). They also agreed to open the account. My father, who is also our organization's registered agent, signed onto the account with me. We received our first personalized debit card and pack of checks; I felt like I was really *adulting* for the first time.

Though it may be difficult to open a bank account at first, it is worth it in the long run, particularly if your nonprofit is a service-based organization. When I shop for care packages or medical supplies for kids with cancer, it's much easier to whip out a debit or credit card that directly links to the funding our organization has. When donating to another organization, it's much more professional to write a check or wire a bank transfer compared to other donation alternatives like using a personal bank account. The latter option requires you to manually track donations and expenses while using Venmo, Cash App, and PayPal under your personal name. All expenses would also have to come out of pocket. An organization bank account makes it easier for your nonprofit to track expenses and revenue and plan budgets for upcoming years.

When you're looking for which bank to open an account with, pay attention to the fine print. Certain banks like Bank of America will charge a monthly fee if you do not maintain a certain amount of money in your account or hit a certain number of transactions per month. For nonprofits starting out, this financial loss can be harmful!

Choosing the right bank is just one of many foundational decisions you'll make early on. As you begin to build out your nonprofit, you'll realize that every part of it, from managing finances to running programs, depends on one key thing: your people.

4

Assembling the Nonprofit Superteam

STARTING A NONPROFIT might feel like stepping into uncharted territory—but you're not meant to do it alone. Having a committed and exceptional leadership team behind you can propel your organization to great heights. In the wise words of Michael Jordan, "Talent wins games, but teamwork . . . wins championships." Think of it like building your own squad of superheroes—just like the Avengers or the Justice League, your nonprofit superteam will bring together people with different strengths, talents, and passions to help you tackle big challenges and make real change.

But let's be real—at the ripe age of *teenager,* how do you build and manage a team that's just as dedicated to your cause as you are? How do you find people who share your vision, hold them accountable, and ensure that everyone is working together effectively? And, perhaps the biggest challenge of all, how do you lead your peers without coming across as overbearing or bossy?

This chapter will walk you through the process of assembling your dream team and creating a leadership structure and style that allows your nonprofit to thrive. Because at the end of the day, the success of your organization is dependent on the collective strength of the people you surround yourself with.

Building *the* Team

At fourteen, I had no idea what it meant to "build a team." Naively, I only wanted my friends to join my nonprofit's leadership team because all I was thinking about was how *fun* it would be to work with my friends. It was also a great excuse to convince my mom to let us hang out together if she thought we were planning events instead of wasting time at the shopping mall.

Cancer Kids First's founding team consisted of me as the CEO, Emily as the secretary, and Taylor as the treasurer (names have been changed for privacy reasons). For the first six months, we were a dynamic team. Every lunch break, we would park ourselves in our school's courtyard and discuss our progress while snacking on carrots and hummus. They were as committed as I was, and working with my friends meant I was spending almost every hour with my favorite people. We celebrated every milestone—from making our first one hundred dollars at a local business bake sale to donating our first hundreds of toys and books to Cincinnati Children's Hospital. When I needed help baking fifty cupcakes to sell, I knew I could call Emily, who would drive over at any hour to fill my kitchen with fluffy vanilla pastries (and she did). When I needed a list of every US pediatric cancer hospital organized by state, Taylor was on it without my asking. Through thick and thin, we went through it all together.

But, the honeymoon period of our founding team eventually came to an end as high school began kicking our butts. Emily was the first to pull away—softball and school began taking up more of her time and priorities. She began missing meetings, hardly ever returned my texts and calls, and failed to turn in her work on time. When I replay these months in my mind, it's like I was watching someone fall out of love: I saw her lose passion for CKF.

It took me a long time to muster the courage to talk to her. I have always been *horrible* at confronting others or standing up for myself, especially in person. At fourteen, how was I supposed to *fire* someone? I had never had to do something like that before; I did not know how many "chances" to give her before finally replacing her or how to communicate the things CKF and I needed. It took me two months to have the conversation with her, and to this day, it is still one of the hardest conversations I have had.

When I was thinking about how fun it would be to work with my friends, it never crossed my mind to reflect on how *firing* one of them would feel. I remember feeling tremendous anxiety leading up to it and rushing through my sentences as I tried to force my concerns out. I looked everywhere but at her. Emily, luckily, was understanding and self-aware: she acknowledged that she had been slacking on her work for the past few months and explained that she could not dedicate the appropriate amount of time or energy to the secretary role due to stress and her workload. She agreed to step down.

It ended as well as it could have, but still, I felt heavy guilt for the next few weeks and tiptoed around her. At lunch, I never brought up the topic of CKF and shielded milestones we had hit because I was worried it would hurt her. It was then that I learned the important lesson of separating your business and personal life.

When you work with a friend, you can put tension on the friendship (as a result of arguments you may have over workload, quality of work, decisions, or changing dynamics where one friend is the "boss" of another).

For example, you might hesitate to give honest feedback or hold your friend accountable when they miss deadlines or underdeliver—not because you don't care about the project, but because you're afraid of hurting their feelings. This can lead to resentment, miscommunication, or one-sided effort that damages both the work and the relationship. Similarly, friends may expect favors ("Can I skip this meeting?") or special treatment, which can lead to distrust within your team. Groupthink and bias could also manifest, as teams made of close friends might discourage disagreement or honest critique; people don't want to be the "bad guy," which limits growth and innovation.

It also becomes difficult for you to draw boundaries in your professional and personal life. During my high school years, CKF became so intertwined with everything I did that I had no physical or mental break from the organization; I couldn't separate the people in my life or the time I had for friends, schoolwork, and CKF because it was all intermingled. This is the quickest way to cause burnout. It's important to give your mind and body a break from work by establishing a home-school-work separation. This way, you will feel excited by the chance to work on your nonprofit again and can focus wholeheartedly on each sector of your life.

For instance, today, although I consider many of CKF's current team members to be close friends of mine, I don't see them every day at school or hang out with them much outside of work environments. This gives me the opportunity to shut off the "CKF" side of my brain when I'm with friends or family or focused on school.

If you end up working with a friend, think about implementing boundaries like limiting work talk outside of "working hours" and emphasizing that work decisions are based on performance rather than personal relationships. Avoid favoritism and give constructive feedback when necessary, embracing any changes to the friendship that may be inevitable with the roles.

When it comes to the actual positions that will compose your leadership team, the following are recommended ideas for leadership positions you can look to fill. (Note: there is no one "title" you can assign these positions, but "officer" is a term often used both within nonprofits and in business, as well as in IRS forms, because it creates needed accountability by denoting who is responsible for certain critical functions.) The starred positions (★) are required for legal forms when filing for nonprofit status, and the **bolded positions** are core members of a beginner team.

- ★ **Chief executive officer/president:** Engages in strategic planning, management, and advocacy for the organization; oversees all directors and departments; builds and maintains relationships with partners and supporters; works with board to adhere to mission and vision; represents organization

★ **Chief financial officer/treasurer:** Creates annual budget and expense/revenue sheet for financial planning; ensures financial transparency; develops financial strategies to maximize impact; conducts audit; works with CEO on strategy and organization initiatives

★ **Chief operations officer/secretary:** Files government forms and ensures organization compliance with nonprofit laws; manages administrative and operational functions; works with CEO on strategy and organization initiatives

▸ **Events director:** Creates, plans, and spearheads events

▸ Fundraising director: Creates, plans, and spearheads fundraisers

▸ Service program lead (e.g., tutoring director) or team lead: Leads respective service programs for service-based organizations or teams for other types of nonprofits

▸ **Social media, communications, or outreach director:** Designs posts, stories, and captions for social media; answers DMs; grows followers; handles influencer partnerships; interacts with other accounts

▸ Partnership director: Comes up with partnership ideas; hosts meetings and facilitates communication with prospective partners; heads partnership initiatives

▸ Human resources manager: Facilitates a fun team environment and member retention by hosting meetings, workshops, games, and parties; onboards and fires directors; establishes director performance evaluations and goal setting; runs organization recognition program; fosters DEI

▸ Volunteer coordinator: Handles service hours and communication with volunteers

- ▸ Grant director: Applies for government, company, and nonprofit grants
- ▸ Chapter director: Trains and onboards all chapters; reviews updates and tracks chapter progress; organizes chapter network (if you choose to start a chapter or ambassador program)

When you're building your founding team, the two other officers (chief financial officer/treasurer and chief operations officer/secretary) are the pillars that are going to support and uplift your organization. To this day, I am still incredibly close with my organization's chief operations officer, Nidhi Sathyanarayanan. She transformed the operations aspect of our organization when we took off in 2021. She came to our organization with a dedication I had never seen before: each weekend, we stayed up well past midnight, filtering and interviewing volunteer and chapter director candidates over FaceTime—even when that went far beyond her required work hours. She was the first person I texted when I came up with new service programs, partnerships, or event ideas (yes, I did blow up her phone with over twenty texts at 3:00 a.m.), and she never hesitated to add details she thought of to improve my initial action plans. I don't think I've ever heard a "no" come out of her mouth; she took on every task I handed her with enthusiasm and always exceeded my expectations. Plus, she backed me up in meetings, outreached to her network when we needed resources, and supplied pep talks when I needed them. I can't credit Nidhi enough for the positive turn our organization has taken. The right person can truly turn your organization around for the better.

The chief operations officer and chief financial officer are your right hands, so think wisely about who you select for these positions. My story with Emily and Taylor isn't to say you shouldn't choose your friends, because these people are likely those you know well and can trust, but think carefully about the pros and cons of working with a friend. Don't pick someone for the sake of convenience!

CHECKLIST FOR THE PERFECT COFOUNDER/RIGHT HAND (A LOT OF THESE CAN BE APPLICABLE TO GENERAL TEAM MEMBERS AS WELL)

☐ They share your values: the most sustainable work relationships are those between people who have similar values (e.g., you both value commitment, even when it's hard, like driving across town to meet with donors or staying up late until a project gets done). If you and your closest team can't agree on goals or a vision, your nonprofit will crumble.

☐ They complement you: I believe the best team consists of members who have skill sets in different areas and can balance one another out. You definitely shouldn't be managing every part of your organization, but every part does need to run smoothly, so having a person who complements you guarantees that any gaps you have can be filled by others. Plus, this way, you can learn far more from your colleagues—and teach them a skill or two! Start with self-awareness. What are your strengths and weaknesses? If you're a visionary, look for someone who will ask the hard logistical questions. Seek values alignment, not skill duplication.

☐ They have experience: this doesn't necessarily mean you need to pick someone who's started or worked at a nonprofit before. Rather, look for someone who has shown the ability to be responsible, take initiative, go above and beyond, and handle pressure. This can be demonstrated through starting a club, succeeding academically, thriving in an after-school program, or practicing everyday habits.

☐ They believe in you and your organization: you cannot build an organization with people who don't believe you can do it. Make sure whoever you bring on will be there cheering you on when things get rough instead of giving up and turning their back on you.

☐ They have resources or added value: obviously, a cofounder or right hand is a greater asset when they can bring something to the table. Do they have industry connections? A knack for designing graphics? An unwavering commitment to finishing a task once they start? If your organization were a puzzle, each team member would be like a puzzle piece. They must fit into the overall culture and environment but also bring something of substance to contribute to the overall picture.

☐ They believe in communication, communication, communication: You *cannot* work well with someone who is bad at communicating. You need to be able to properly discuss ideas, conduct meetings, resolve conflicts, and provide/receive constructive criticism.

When put together, your nonprofit superteam should also be diverse. Collaborate across different backgrounds (age, race, and experience), personality types, and more. People who complement you won't always agree with you, but that's a good thing!

As a young person, you most likely have a network of other young people you can reach out to and invite to join your nonprofit's leadership team. Simple communities where you can start your outreach include your school, sports teams, and extracurricular clubs. These communities are great because they can help you assess your peers' dedication levels and passions before introducing a leadership position opportunity. For instance, top athletes are often very goal-driven people who excel at time management because they have had to implement those skill sets in their sports. Prior club officers, like people who have done yearbook, Model UN, or the school newspaper, can have great experience and tangible skills to help with a nonprofit. Keeping these traits in mind can help guide you in choosing people to join your leadership team.

Aside from direct outreach, you can also find leadership directors by cold-messaging people on LinkedIn. Take some time to look through your connections and recommended connections; glance at what your peers have been involved in, and don't be afraid to reach out regarding your nonprofit opportunity to like-minded individuals who share your interests. School and extracurricular activities can physically limit the number of young people you can invite to join your team, but platforms like LinkedIn can serve as a way to broaden your scope while giving you a sneak peek into an individual's résumé.

Another effective way to build your leadership team is to identify volunteers who consistently show up. Shrusti and Rise N Shine do exactly this. One of Rise N Shine's programs to fight food insecurity is a pop-up pantry, where her organization's members gather in a central location to prepare groceries for individuals in need. Shrusti believes her leadership team should be composed of other young people that share her passion and vision, so she notes down volunteers who consistently show up and show out at their events. She then invites the most dedicated team members to join her in leadership.

Constructing a leadership team this way can be extremely effective because you already know that the candidate is someone who is familiar with your organization, will put in the time and effort needed, and fits in with the dynamics of your team. It almost "fills in" the need for an interview.

Whether you have a network in place that you can already reach out to, I recommend creating and distributing an application form (on Google Forms, Typeform, Jotform, or another application platform) that assesses personal qualities and professional work fit. Questions like the following are always great to bring out someone's character and see if they can follow directions:

- ▸ Choose three words that best describe your (1) work ethic, (2) personality, and (3) social skills and explain why. Limit responses to one hundred words each.

- ▸ What are you most proud of? This can be an accomplishment, a character trait, a story, etc. (no more than 200 words).

Once you create a leadership application, consider sharing it on social media to reach a wider demographic. For instance, Sophia Kianni, the Iranian American climate activist, posted announcements on Instagram, Facebook, Twitter, and even TikTok. Each post directed viewers to the written leadership team application on their website, along with a request for a résumé and relevant experience in the environmental sector. Sophia asked current team members and friends to repost the announcements to expand the circle of people aware of Climate Cardinals' leadership opportunities. There is something to be said for broadening the locations from which your leadership team members come because while that makes setting meeting times harder, it also means you have a larger pool of potential partners, volunteers, and resources. Geographically diverse leadership team members can also bring new insights and perspectives, as location can influence our culture, beliefs, attitudes, and more.

Next, scheduling an interview is a key step to ensure that candidates are both qualified and a good fit for your team's dynamic. One of my favorite questions to ask is about their 16 Personalities (MBTI) quiz result and what they think it reveals about themselves. I also like to pose a scenario-based question—"Pretend you're in this situation . . ."—to see how they think on their feet and handle challenges.

As your organization begins scaling in size and impact, you may also want to implement a trial week as the last step in joining the leadership team. This, perhaps, is the most vital step because it allows you and your team to see if someone truly has the work ethic and knowledge they claim to have. It's often easy for someone to present themselves well through a Google Form application or interview, but backing those words up with actions is hard. For instance, if they're applying to be a fundraising director, you can ask them to send over a list of fundraisers and draft an email of what they would send to a proposed company or organization.

Sometimes, when you're stuck between two great candidates, it can be helpful to ask the rest of your team for opinions. Furthermore, think about whether their personality would add something to the team environment, and consider diversity (gender, race, and background) and retention (even if a candidate is perfect, if they're only going to stay for a few months because they leave for college soon, it's not worth it!). It's also a great idea to keep a database or note of qualified candidates who may not have been selected for the final position but would be a good fit for other positions in the future.

Board of Directors

Aside from your leadership team, you will also need a board of directors. This may sound a little daunting, but I'm going to break it down for you. Each nonprofit organization is required to elect a minimum of three adults who are not related to each other to serve on the board of directors. There are a few options for creating this board. You could ask your parents or your classmates' parents, reach out to connections you have, or cold-email (messaging someone you have had no prior relationship with) industry professionals.

While it may seem more convenient to ask your parents or friends' parents to serve on your board, in the long run, seeking industry professionals will shape your organization's impact and strategy. They can give leadership advice when you face team conflicts, shape your events and fundraisers, share presentation tips, refocus your team, and set goals for you to achieve. Think of them like experienced members who can guide your nonprofit leadership and strategy.

Consider looking for nonprofit professionals, company CEOs, or executives in your nonprofit's field (e.g., if you are working in the climate field, reach out to environmental activists or policymakers who focus on green energy). You can find these individuals through Google Search, LinkedIn, or social media. You can also search for board members based on the skills you need, whether it's legal help (a lawyer) or grant support (a fundraising head). To make the process of creating the board of directors easier, your team can create a simple table listing the skills, experiences, and perspectives you're looking for. As you recruit board members, track how each person adds to the mix. This helps avoid stacking the board with similar types of people. Unlike a leadership team, your board of directors can remain small. Think quality over quantity!

Here's an example pitch email to get you started:

SUBJECT: Board Invitation: Uplift Young Leaders and Support the Childhood Cancer Community

Dear Ms./Mr. _____,

My name is Olivia Zhang, and I am the CEO and founder of Cancer Kids First, a 501(c)(3) dedicated to normalizing the hospital environment and providing a community for kids with cancer. We are the world's largest youth-led nonprofit uniting over 40,000 volunteers in 80 countries and have impacted 10,000 patients in 22 countries.

I greatly admire your leadership at _____ and your exceptional skills in _____ [personal detail]. We would love to invite you to serve on our Board of Directors; current board members include a UPenn professor and successful executives at other nonprofits.

The time commitment would only be an hour (virtually) every quarter and would accommodate your schedule. If you're unable to commit to board meetings, we'd love to receive your mentorship over email/text communication as well!

Thank you for your time and consideration. I can meet to provide more details if that would be helpful, or feel free to send me questions! If you are unable to serve on our board, perhaps you could send us names of others we can ask.

Sincerely,
Olivia

With a robust and high-profile board, your nonprofit and team will be equipped with professionals who can offer incredible guidance and advice to steer your organization in the right direction. While the previous chapter explored the importance of mission statements, it's just as important to define where you're headed. That's where a strong vision statement comes in—and a good board can be instrumental in helping you shape it.

A mission statement defines *what* your organization does, *who* it serves, and *how* it does it—essentially, your nonprofit's purpose today. It should be clear, action-oriented, and grounded in your current work. On the other hand, a vision statement describes *what success looks like* in the future if your mission is fulfilled. It's aspirational and forward looking, painting a picture of the change you want to see in the world. Let's say you want to start a nonprofit to support immigrants. A mission statement could be something like "To empower immigrant youth and families by providing culturally sensitive mentorship, language support, and community integration resources—led by students, for students." A vision statement would then be "A society where immigrant youth feel welcomed, supported, and equipped to thrive academically, socially, and emotionally in their new home."

Board members can help you craft a mission and vision statement, ensuring that your organization's actions stay true to the mission and move toward the vision. Try to mix strategic and supportive board members to have some members be strategic thinkers who help guide the big picture, while others roll up their sleeves to help complete action items.

Take the time to develop your board, and as your organization progresses, continuously seek board members in areas of interest!

That Team Environment

We've all heard the quote "It's the people that make the place," and this has never rung truer than for a nonprofit organization. Your organization will only be successful if you have leadership directors, volunteers, and supporters who are equally as passionate about the mission as you are. They need to be excited to come to work every day, and it is up to you to ignite that spark.

Establishing clear roles and expectations is the first priority in cultivating a strong team environment. From the top of the pyramid (you, as the founder, and the other leadership directors) to the bottom (volunteers and members), team members must understand their responsibilities and feel purposeful in the work they do to be productive and stay engaged.

While I briefly covered leadership roles you may want your nonprofit to have, we cannot forget about the roles of volunteers in the organization. It's hard to provide a specific reference for this since every organization's volunteer roles depend on the mission itself, but there are a few general principles to keep in mind when designating volunteer roles.

LiteratureDiversified is a youth-led nonprofit working to diversify school curricula and foster more inclusive classrooms for underrepresented students worldwide. Led by Saawan Duvvuri, the team has created over 450 educational resources across seventy lesson plans, workshops, and research collections. Their work has earned recognition from the Prudential Emerging Visionaries, the Ashoka Foundation, the Princeton Prize in Race Relations, and NBC's *Today Show*.

The organization operates through four core volunteer teams, each aligned with their mission to advance racial equity in education:

- ► **Curriculum Team:** Develops inclusive K–12 resources in pods such as US History, Literature, Financial Literacy, and Social Action, ensuring content meets state standards (developing your core service)
- ► **Outreach & Partnerships:** Connects with educators, schools, and global chapters to implement curricula and build partnerships (partnering with schools or local chapters)

- **Policy & Advocacy:** Researches disparities in education policy and collaborates with legislative youth councils (driving systemic change)

- **Communications & Media:** Manages branding, social media, video content, and the website (telling your story)

This structure is a great model for youth-led nonprofits. You can organize volunteers based on

- **Core activities**: What your organization does

- **Impact pipelines**: How your work reaches your audience

Another approach is based on functional roles:

- **Fundraising**: Organizing donation drives and campaigns

- **Marketing**: Designing and managing social media

- **Outreach**: Building partnerships and handling external emails

- **Administration**: Supporting tech, operations, and logistics

- **Event engagement**: Planning and running events

Or, for service-based nonprofits like Letters to Strangers, your teams may reflect programs directly:

- **Service Program A** (e.g., letter writing)

- **Content & Curriculum** (e.g., education resources)

- **Advocacy & Research** (e.g., policy change)

Once you've defined your volunteer structure, consider how you'll recruit for each role. Refer to the marketing chapters for recruitment strategies.

The most important consideration when assigning volunteer roles is ensuring they align with each volunteer's skills, interests, and strengths. How will your team allocate volunteers? Will there be some sort of interview or assessment process, or will you give your volunteers the freedom to choose based on what they're interested in? No matter which option you choose, ensure you write clear and detailed descriptions of the volunteer roles. Include the responsibilities, expected time commitment, skills required, and impact on the nonprofit's mission. If you choose to break your volunteers into teams, each team should have its own project lead, and team members should be given consistent but flexible roles—whether that's weekly research tasks, monthly campaign deadlines, or biweekly team calls—to keep them engaged and accountable. This structure allows for scalability, leadership development, and deep impact across different areas of the organization. Implement efforts to regularly check in with volunteers as well; volunteer retention largely depends on volunteers feeling comfortable and fulfilled in their roles. For larger organizations, it is especially important not to forget this. You want to adjust appropriately if volunteers are not engaged or satisfied with being part of your organization. A small but involved team is much more effective than a large but inactive team!

That leads right into the creation of a team environment. Think about what it would be like if you were a new student joining a class. You'd probably want to be welcomed and supported, especially in the beginning stages. This is the same mindset for new team members. It can be something as simple as sending a welcome text in your team's group chat or creating a slideshow to introduce the new team member during a team meeting.

Time and time again, employees cite the company environment and recognition as prime reasons for employee retention. Brainstorm ways with your officers and directors to make working on your nonprofit's team fulfilling *and* fun—especially in virtual environments. Here are some ways nonprofits do it!

BIRTHDAY TEXTS AND SOCIAL MEDIA SHOUT-OUTS: It's a small way to ensure your team knows that you remember them on their special day.

ANNUAL PRIZES (TROPHIES, MERCH, TREATS, OR GIFT CARDS) FOR TOP PERFORMERS: It motivates everyone to work as hard as they can while recognizing those who go above and beyond.

IMPACT PICTURES OR INSPIRATIONAL QUOTES: Sending pictures of the impact your team has made on others will motivate them to continue pushing; inspirational quotes can help direct their mindset and serve as a bonding activity!

TEAM MEETINGS AND EVENTS: Goes without saying . . . but make these fun with icebreakers and interactive games! Breakout rooms can be a fun way to bring together directors who don't typically work with one another.

REFLECTION AND GOAL WORKSHEETS: Ensuring your team reflects on their past performance and sets new goals for themselves every quarter or year is critical to cultivating their leadership skills.

RANDOM TEXTS: One of the cutest moments I saw in my nonprofit was when one of our chapter directors texted our group chat asking for advice for a first date . . . the feedback she got was so heartwarming!!! It really brought our team together and showed both me and the other members that we didn't need to have a strictly professional relationship; it also showed how we were always there for each other in times of uncertainty or need.

Once you've made your leadership team selections, make sure you design training sessions for the directors so they fully understand their roles and responsibilities. Segment them into position-specific roles and general leadership team roles. For example, on top of their position's tasks, you could require all leadership directors to engage with social media posts, participate in a certain number of events and fundraisers every year, and attend quarterly leadership team meetings. Clearly outline these requirements for new team members so there is no confusion about what is expected of them moving forward and so everyone is held to the same standard.

If you are onboarding a new team member who is replacing a current director, it can be a good idea to connect the new director with the outgoing one so they can gain tips and pick up on the work that remains.

Also, consider asking the outgoing director to create a training document or slideshow for the new team member to make the onboarding process easier.

Another great idea is to establish some sort of mentorship system where the new director has a partner—a current director—who can answer their questions and check over their assignments. This can ensure no one feels thrown into work without appropriate guidance.

Navigating Team Conflicts

No team is perfect. Even after working together for years, colleagues can still get into disagreements that lead to workplace tension. That's why conflict resolution is a very important skill to have. To be a great leader, you have to know how to deal with difficult people, empathize with others, and find common ground. However, having these skills as a teen or tween is hard: most of the time, we don't have to deal with major conflicts, aside from petty arguments on the playground or beefs between friends. Ultimately, the best way to cultivate these skills is through experience. I've put together some of the most common conflicts that may arise and strategies for dealing with them:

BATTLE BETWEEN BRAINS: Conflict between two directors can often occur, particularly when they are partners or work alongside one another. As the leader of both, you have to foster workplace collaboration and ensure both sides feel heard, with neither favored over the other.

In establishing our first chapter in Africa, I selected two aspiring medical students who displayed the drive and knowledge needed to successfully lead an international chapter. However, after our initial conversation, I did not receive any word from them for weeks. One individual—let's call her Lizzie—then informed me of rising tensions with her partner—let's call her Lauren—after the latter had curtailed her involvement in the chapter's social media accounts. Lizzie requested to lead the chapter independently.

When I spoke to Lauren, her plight mirrored Lizzie's. Each refused to work with the other, and both wanted to lead the chapter. I gathered my officer team to explain the situation and collect suggestions and subsequently met individually with Lizzie and Lauren. In both calls, I reiterated the CKF board's admiration for both individuals. But, I also warned that if they couldn't compromise, either by opening communication lines or by focusing on different aspects of the chapter, it would be necessary to select new chapter heads. After all, fulfilling CKF's mission was the top priority. Adhering to my message, Lizzie and Lauren ultimately combined their individual strengths to lead, building their chapter into one of our top chapters.

As outlined in the example, when two directors aren't getting along, you can turn to your mentors or other team members for advice on what to do. When I was growing up, my mom—the CFO of a DC nonprofit—often shared ways she resolved workplace conflict, which helped build my conflict toolkit. Hearing both sides and facilitating communication are fundamental pillars of resolving issues, so any time two directors are having a conflict, ensure you first listen and then come up with solutions. Try reframing the outcome to unify the two parties (e.g., by explaining that the goal is to create and lead the best chapter) and using the conflict as a teaching moment. You can also initiate bonding activities, since it's often easier to work with another person after you understand them outside the professional environment!

THE SLACKER: Every time a new person joins your team, they will most often start out with fervent energy, ready and excited to tackle their new job. However, as months and years go by, they may start to lose motivation and passion. The signs will start with a minor assignment being turned in late or a missed meeting but then can snowball into unanswered emails, multiple missing assignments, and decreased work quality. I think of it like a downward sloping curve (see figure 2).

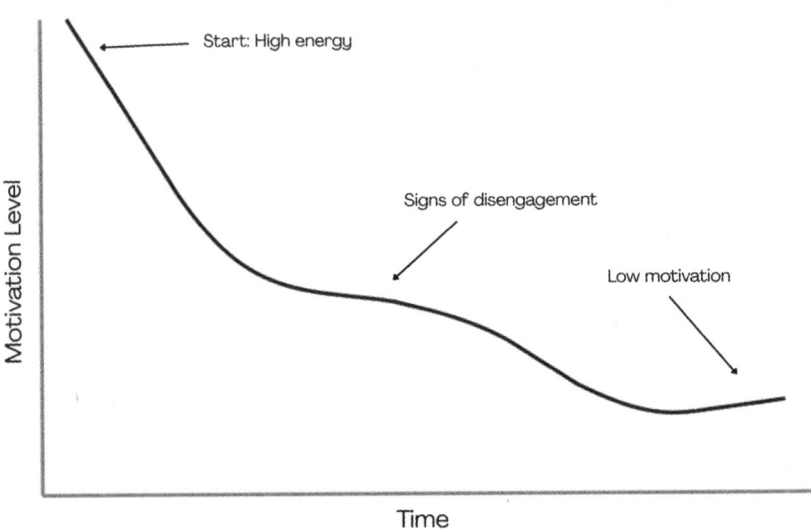

Employee Motivation Over Time

FIGURE 2: Slacker curve. *Source: Ava Zhang. Used with permission.*

This is completely normal. It's human nature to experience declines in motivation and commitment. However, if one of your team members' performance is affecting the overall organization or other team members (e.g., you have to take on more responsibilities or other team members have to shoulder some of their workload to get tasks done on time), you need to take action.

As scary as it can be, communication is key. Reach out to the director in a strict but understanding manner. Seek to uncover what is driving the decline in their work quality, and explain what part of their performance is lacking and the consequences (and be as specific as possible). I like to embody the "steel and velvet" leadership style. Steel ensures you hold your team members accountable; they need to view you as a leader in order to listen to and follow your instructions. At the same time, you must balance that hard exterior with velvet, meaning you must build trust and relationships to be a successful leader.

In this situation, you must firmly stand your ground in order to get that director to step up their work (or even fire them if it hits a breaking point). Yet, you should also try to understand the obstacles they might be facing (final exams, academic pressure, family struggles, etc.) that could influence their work performance. Being able to hear them out will enable you to build a deeper bond with them. This skill is known as empathy, which is generally regarded as the act of putting yourself in the other person's shoes to experience their world.

Every nonprofit leader has had to deal with a slacker. It's the worst when they don't give you a heads-up and completely disappear from the face of the earth—they don't answer your countless texts or calls, leaving you and the rest of your team to deal with their unfinished work. To mitigate this, when you first notice a missing assignment or late work submission, emphasize the importance of contributing equally to the team's success. If their performance doesn't improve after two more communications, send a potential termination text outlining what is expected of them if they want to stay in your organization (aka the "three strikes and you're out!" rule).

Toward the beginning of CKF, I faced a situation with a director who I had sent a few texts to explaining my frustration with her work performance. Because of my lack of experience at that point, I didn't give her a chance to redeem herself. I had made up my mind that we had to fire her. However, she pleaded with me to discuss her side of the story over the phone. I am extremely thankful every day that I took that phone call because I learned valuable lessons that day. First, I realized how scary it is to *tell* someone their faults and hold your ground when you can hear their reactions (I literally hid in my closet during the phone call because my heart was beating so fast). Second, I learned that you have to be willing to give people second chances, especially when your gut instinct tells you to do so (your body tells you a lot!). I had been discontented with this director's performance for a while—she hardly ever responded to my texts and failed to update me on her work each week—which is why I had originally been set on firing her straightaway. But, after hearing her promises to do better moving forward and the actionable steps she would take to resolve her mistakes, I kept her on the team but adjusted her role slightly to better suit her skill set. Today, she has improved immensely in fulfilling her duties and adding to our team environment, whether through sharing her thoughts at team meetings or engaging in events.

HFIRING SOMEONE: Similar to the slacker situation, firing someone can be the toughest thing in the world to do. It can obviously cause a lot of hurt, anger, and even resentment from the other party. Thus, I've created a mini checklist to help you navigate the treacherous waters of firing someone.

YES, YOU SHOULD FIRE THEM IF

- ☐ They do not add value to your organization.

- ☐ They repeatedly turn in work late or with mistakes, despite many warnings.

- ☐ They are rude or disrespectful to you and other team members.

- ☐ They do not believe in you or your organization's mission statement.

FRAMEWORK FOR *THE* CONVERSATION

- ☐ Ensure you prepare materials for "proof" in case there are rebuttals or negative emotions.

- ☐ Be direct in the introduction: explain that the decision is to terminate their position due to XYZ reasons.

- ☐ Provide *specific* examples of performance or behavior issues, along with examples of situations where you or other team members tried to help.

☐ Discuss the termination or transition process: Should they be responsible for training the next individual? Passing down account information? Completing any leftover assignments?

☐ Allow for questions and provide support moving forward, whether by sharing alternative organizations for them to join or by offering to be a reference for future jobs. You always want to end on a good note!

Though firing someone can really be what's best for your organization, it's also understandable that it will weigh on your conscience. You may be worried that firing that person has ruined the relationship between the two of you, or even that you made a mistake in letting them go. What's important to remember in these situations is the reason why you fired them and that you did so to build your organization's team into the best it can be.

Being a leader means handling tough situations like managing people, which can truly be the most difficult task to take on. Remind yourself that with each challenge you push through, you evolve into a stronger leader and person.

Authenticity in Action

Leadership can feel like an abstract concept—especially for young people who haven't seen it up close. As you've gone through the sections of this chapter, hopefully you have gained a better understanding of the characteristics that make up a good leader. However, there's another avenue I haven't hit on yet: the desire for status. It's easy to think leadership is all about big titles, awards, or being the most confident voice in the room. But real leadership starts and ends with getting your hands dirty to earn respect through hard work. Don't let your ego take over! The best CEOs are the ones who remain grounded and are willing to join their volunteers in the weeds to solve a social issue. The CEOs who are motivated by purpose and belief, rather than by achievement and fame, are also those that are likely to succeed in the long run.

Take Restaurant Brands International as a case study. Restaurant Brands International is one of the world's largest quick-service restaurant companies and owns popular food chains like Burger King, Tim Hortons, and Popeyes.[1] They run an enlightening internship program with a unique characteristic that I believe should be adopted by more companies: interns are required to work at a restaurant, such as Burger King, for a week to understand firsthand the problems they are working to address at a higher level. Restaurant Brands International's method places their interns on the ground so they can see who they are helping and creating change for. They experience all the hardships servers and hosts encounter on the daily, increasing the interns' awareness of prevalent problems and potential solutions.

Similar to Restaurant Brands International, you should do your due diligence by getting into the weeds of your own organization. That could mean putting in a few extra hours to bake cookies for a fundraiser or working alongside your volunteers to design posters for an event. These hands-on experiences will earn your team's respect, set an example for your other directors, and remind you of your humble beginnings.

5

Dollars and Dreams

ONCE YOU'VE ASSEMBLED your nonprofit superteam, the next step is clear: securing the funding you need to support that team and your organization.

Money makes the world—and your nonprofit—go 'round. Without adequate funding, even your most passionate efforts can fall short of making a lasting impact on the communities you aim to serve. For youth-led organizations, raising hundreds of thousands of dollars can feel like an uphill battle, especially when competing with well-established, adult-run nonprofits that have more resources, experience, and connections. But, we can't discount what makes us unique: our ideas, passion, and fervent energy.

Most youth-led nonprofits start from humble beginnings, often relying on small-scale fundraisers. I once heard about a local community organization in my area that began with bake sales. Their small team spent an entire afternoon under the scorching sun, tirelessly selling cookies—only to make a mere $27. Yet, they didn't give up. The following weekend, they set up shop in another neighborhood, relentlessly selling their treats until they made a notable $400. While it was still a small amount, it was certainly an improvement over $27. And that just illustrates the relentless drive young people have. How many adults do you know who would walk in the heat for over eight hours, selling baked goods one by one, just to fund a cause they believe in? Youth-led organizations may not always have the financial backing that larger nonprofits do, but they make up for it with resilience, creativity, and an unwavering commitment to their mission. And that is where real impact begins.

Local Fundraising

When you're first starting out, host in-person team fundraisers like lemonade stands and bake sales. While simple, these can introduce your nonprofit to the local community and strengthen your team's bond.

One of Cancer Kids First's initial fundraisers was a bake sale held at our local Kumon. We raised only a couple of hundred dollars, but it taught our entire team perseverance and courage. We spent five hours baking and frosting cupcakes. When the day of the fundraiser arrived, we braved the cold and set up camp outside Kumon for the afternoon. Each time someone walked by, we took turns mustering the courage to pitch our organization and ask for donations. That day, I felt tied to my community and team in a way I hadn't before; I recognized the mutual fear that my colleagues and I shared in speaking to strangers. We encouraged each other to step outside our comfort zones. At the same time, we learned and refined our nonprofit pitching skills by analyzing what got someone to buy a cupcake versus walking away. Starting from these "scrappy" beginnings makes it all the more worthwhile to see your team and money grow! Plus, it was heartwarming to see how many Kumon students, families, and workers were willing to support our cause.

Other local fundraiser ideas include a car wash, a yard sale, dog walking, auctions, product sales (anything from art to customized clothing), and a movie or game night. You'll notice that many of these require a team of volunteers to organize and set up the event. It's costly, both in time and human capital, but it also solidifies that feeling of community—and that is core to a strong youth-led organization in its initial stages.

Another option is to approach local businesses, religious institutions, or other charitable organizations to ask for donations either in person or over the phone. Utilize the elevator pitch we covered in chapter 2—explaining why you started your nonprofit, the problem you've identified that needs to be solved, and your plans to address that problem—and ask for any possible contributions. You'd be surprised how many people are willing to help out just after hearing an authentic story!

National Fundraising

When you've grown your nonprofit to a national level, you can begin branching out your fundraising efforts to include less fieldwork while reaching a broader range of donors. Most of these fundraisers should also be virtual to allow for increased participation.

There are a lot of opportunities to explore partnerships with businesses. For instance, you can reach out to partner with food chains like Chipotle and Panda Express to have a certain percentage of their profits donated to your organization on a specific day. Similarly, Kendra Scott is a philanthropic business that hosts "in-kind events," where your nonprofit's supporters can use an online code or come into a physical location to purchase products, while the business donates 20 percent of the profits made. In a different vein, there are companies like Double Good, Neighbors Cookies, and Super Fan Fundraising that focus on helping nonprofits and other community organizations raise money. For these fundraisers, you and your team sell the company's products (e.g., popcorn for Double Good) and receive a certain percentage of the profits. It can be really rewarding and fun, since many of these companies have built-in apps with leaderboards and communication functions that encourage every member to sell as many products as possible. They also streamline the payout process since their company model is centered on increasing donations for charitable causes. Double Good, in particular, is worth exploring, as its fundraising platform is geared toward large youth groups.

Other options for national fundraisers include virtual raffles, virtual movie nights with an entry fee, power hours (volunteers send out texts and emails to their networks for donations during a set time), Google Ads grants that promote your organization in search results, and virtual walk-a-thons (money can be collected through an entry fee or by sponsoring each mile a volunteer walks).

If you have a fairly large social media presence, you can translate this visibility into funding by sharing your fundraisers online and asking your followers to participate. Even something as simple as creating a GoFundMe and sharing the link when you see your social media platform gaining traction can help raise funds. Bonus points if you capitalize on current events (e.g., a hurricane disaster striking XYZ town and you're a disaster relief organization) or national awareness months (e.g., Breast Cancer Awareness Month). For instance, on a walk home from Mass General during the pandemic, Natalie Guo—an investor at Thrive Capital and the founder of the nonprofit Off Their Plate—saw that the restaurants on Charles Street had shut down and laid off their staff. At the same time, she knew that hospital workers were eating from vending machines because grocery stores were out of stock and restaurants had closed. To bridge the gap, she started a PayPal pool to provide wages for restaurant workers who would make hot meals for hospital workers instead. She sent the link to her circle of friends and, to her surprise, woke up the next morning with $30,000 in the fund. People were eager to help, either by donating or by sharing the PayPal pool, and they responded to the immediacy and call to action.

Big Leagues: Grants and Awards

Once your organization has gone national or even international, you may want to consider applying for grants. Grants can come from the government, businesses, or other nonprofits. Sometimes, grant funding comes with strings attached and is applicable only to certain types of nonprofits (e.g., only nonprofits in the STEM sector or those helping the environment). For instance, if the grant comes from a small nonprofit in Connecticut, it may require you to spend the money they give you only on helping patients in Connecticut. Through grant databases and by googling phrases like "environmental grants," you can find general grants for nonprofits or those specific to the field your nonprofit operates in.

It can be very difficult for youth-led organizations to receive grants since grant givers want to know that their money will be going toward authentic organizations that will achieve true impact. (They operate like a business too! They want to support organizations that will give them the highest return on their investment.) And, unfortunately, adults are more inclined to trust other adults or established organizations. Nevertheless, there are companies that have been known to support youth-led community projects. Here are some examples of grants to look into:

- ▸ Grants.gov (database of federally funded grants)
- ▸ Hershey Heartwarming Action Grant
- ▸ Kars4Kids
- ▸ Pilot G2 Overachievers Student Grant
- ▸ Walmart Foundation
- ▸ Riley's Way Foundation Call for Kindness Grant

Don't limit yourself to youth-centric grants, though. Outcompeting adult-run nonprofits can be difficult, but as conveyed in chapter 2, by authentically sharing your founding story and emphasizing the strengths of your youth-led team, you can overcome the stigma associated with it.

Another great way to collect funding (and mentorship!) to further your project is by applying for social impact awards and competitions. These are often competitive, with an acceptance rate of less than 5 percent, so only those with innovative projects or nonprofits with demonstrated impact should apply. Many applications also require essays, letters of recommendation, images or videos, and transcripts. The following are some examples of national awards for young leaders that provide funding. For local and state opportunities, you can search your local news, scroll through LinkedIn, or reach out to your school.

- L'Oréal Women of Worth: Honors ten exceptional women who "receive $25,000 to support their charitable cause, mentorship from the L'Oréal Paris network and a national platform to tell their stories."[1]

- The Princeton Prize in Race Relations: Recognizes "high school students who, through action and service, have demonstrated leadership in advancing racial equity or promoting racial understanding in their schools and communities."[2] Winners receive an award of $2,500 and are invited to participate in a symposium.

- Rise Fellowship: Identifies individuals "ages 15–17 and encourages a lifetime of service and learning by providing support that includes need-based scholarships, mentorship, networking, access to career development opportunities, and the potential for additional funding as Rise Fellows work toward solving humanity's most pressing problems."[3]

- Gloria Barron Prize for Young Heroes: Awards eight- to eighteen-year-olds "who have made a significant positive difference to people and the environment."[4] The twenty-five winners receive $10,000 and national press recognition to elevate their work.

- Taco Bell Ambition Accelerator: Celebrates changemakers aged 16–26 with cool ideas in partnership with Ashoka. Leaders from the United States and India are eligible to apply; "this is your chance to grow your changemaking abilities, access [$25,000 worth of] funding, receive feedback on your project, discover a community of like-minded young people, and more!"[5]

- NSHSS scholarships: Award funds in various categories, from talent in the arts to STEM. The National Society of High School

Scholars was created to support high-achieving students and offers a few scholarships for demonstrated leadership and community service.

Alternative funding methods that don't require applications include a co-venture agreement. In simple terms, it is an agreement between two nonprofits to sell products, with a percentage of the sales going toward one of the nonprofits.[6] Sawyer Anderson—a fifteen-year-old and the founder of Water Works, a nonprofit providing clean water to those without—partners with Wellspring for the World and World Vision in a co-venture agreement to raise money for building wells in Africa. More specifically, she sells a book she wrote and African wax bags she created to fundraise, and her partners triple the amount she collects. For instance, if she were to fundraise $200 by selling products she created, Wellspring for the World and World Vision would donate $600 to construct wells. Through this agreement, she has raised $1,350,000 to build 94 wells and save 29,000 lives.

If you can find international organizations with established funding bases, you can reach out to support their services and propose a co-venture agreement where they match the amount of donations you raise (or triple it, like in Sawyer's case). This way, you not only gain a partner but also increase your chances of fundraising success to make an impact.

Crafting a Fundraising Campaign

Crowdfunding, which means raising money from a large number of people through an online platform, can be a strategy for youth-led organizations to implement. Crowdfunding allows nonprofits to reach donors outside their network since online fundraising platforms encourage supporters to share the campaign, bringing organic visibility to the nonprofit. Young people, especially, understand the digital world and how social media can catapult stories and messages, so use your knowledge and love for technology to bring in that money!

Popular crowdfunding platforms for nonprofits include GoFundMe, GoFundMe Pro, Givebutter, and Fundly. All encourage you to set a clear, attainable goal and include high-quality images and videos to tell a compelling story.

In my Economics of Development and Global Health class, I was introduced to a concept that forever changed how I think about fundraising: salience refers to what's important or what tends to jump out at us. Because our brains have limited capacity, we tend to focus on what's emotionally striking or easy to visualize, while tuning out large-scale issues that impact entire populations. According to Professor Matthew Basilico, a physician-economist at Harvard, our brains use this filter to conserve energy. While helpful from an evolutionary standpoint, this limitation can have unfortunate consequences. When we're overwhelmed by statistics or distant suffering, we tend to disengage—not because we don't care, but because we literally don't have the mental capacity to connect with everyone.

This closely connects with the work of British anthropologist Robin Dunbar, who theorized that we can maintain stable, meaningful social relationships with only about 150 people—a concept now known as Dunbar's number. That's roughly 150 people whose lives we can actively keep track of. When we hear about a nameless group of children affected by a disease in a country we've never been to, it feels distant. But when we're introduced to just one child, with a name, a face, and a story, something shifts. That child enters our emotional orbit—becoming one of "our 150"—and suddenly, we care.

This has powerful implications for fundraising. People are far more likely to donate when presented with a specific, personal story than with broad statistics. You need to make the invisible seem visible and the abstract feel personal. Take this example: if you read about Rebecca, a five-year-old battling a life-threatening illness, and her journey until she passed away, you would naturally feel connected to her and her family. The empathy that this personal story sparked may inspire you to donate money or volunteer at a hospital to support other kids going through this disease. On the other hand, if you read about a dozen unnamed children who died from the same life-threatening disease, you would probably feel a hint of sadness but be less inclined to actually *do something* to help. We humans are generally selfish creatures, and the way to pull at our heartstrings involves making a problem relevant to us.

Thus, when designing fundraisers, think about highlighting one specific person or group that your organization has supported or is intending to support. Instead of a general tagline like "Donate to aid kids with cancer," share pictures and personal information about who the money is going to and why it's important to donate now (e.g., she just finished chemotherapy and requires a trampoline for her physical therapy recovery journey). You can even try out both call-to-action methods and watch salience in action!

6

Branding Yourself and Your Story

LEARNING TO BRAND YOURSELF is a powerful tool in many settings, and for a nonprofit founder, branding and storytelling are critical to success. Nonprofits are special in that they rely on emotional connection, credibility, and community support to drive donations, volunteerism, and advocacy. By putting serious effort into creating a compelling brand and story, your organization will stand out.

Marketing

Growing any organization is hard, especially a youth-led organization. In late 2019, Cancer Kids First started with just three members in Virginia, but by 2021, we had grown to 10,000 members in 27 countries. The growth was unprecedented. Today, we stand at 40,500-plus members in 80 countries. How did we get here?

The first step was spreading awareness of our organization throughout my high school. I created a social media account, texted and emailed all my friends (Gmail even blocked my email address after I sent multiple rounds of 500 emails . . .), and reached out to my school administration to hang up flyers. My high school was part of a pyramid of schools—meaning we had "sibling" elementary and middle schools—so I reached out to those schools as well to share flyers or digital newsletters and invite students to join our mission. I vividly remember stuffing flyers I had created into hundreds of students' take-home folders with our initial team of volunteers. It took us four hours.

You can reach out to your district or nearby elementary, middle, and high schools (and even colleges!) to ask if their principals are willing to share an infographic or email blurb about your organization. Consider sharing different volunteer or donation opportunities to ensure you have a clear call to action. Make sure you include a QR code or something easy to direct viewers to your organization.

Another way to grow your organization's volunteer base is to utilize platforms like Idealist, GivePulse, and Points of Light. For instance, Idealist connects nonprofits with volunteers interested in service-hour opportunities. You can create an account for your organization to post any open events or projects that you need volunteers for. Your posting will then be readily available to volunteers nationwide. On your posting, be sure to include a website or social media account to check out, as that can help you retain volunteers for future events.

However, to reach growth quickly, there is no better marketing tool than social media. TikTok and Instagram Reels are perhaps the two best platforms to try out; they are very similar in nature and give new, smaller accounts the opportunity to go viral. It costs no money to use them, and sometimes, the most random videos can go viral. But, in my experience, understanding the algorithms and trends is important to ensure success. If you decide to create an account, plan in advance the first five videos you're going to post and conduct in-depth research on them. Pick a niche (e.g., sharing tips on XYZ or filming videos on how to get service hours through your organization) and curate your account around that theme. Looking at accounts like the one you intend to create can help you come up with video ideas and understand text formatting and music usage. Scrolling through the apps will also help you understand how to word your videos, what kinds of music are popular at the moment, and the best way to edit clips because you get a taste of what's already trending on the platform.

TikTok boosts new accounts because they want you to stay on the app, but if they see your videos are getting limited interaction, they will stop putting them on the "For You" page. You can either film the videos yourself or invite others to join your team as social media directors. For the latter, you need to ensure the candidates you select understand how to use the platform; are comfortable being in front of the camera; understand lighting, quality, and appearance necessities (depending on the niche, certain videos go more viral if you're dressed or acting a certain way); and are creative.

Layla Bizri, our TikTok director, posted our first TikTok video in January 2021, amassing over 1.5 million views. She said that staying consistent on the app—for instance, setting timers for posting every day—was a big reason our account went viral and gained the following it did. She also noted that social media directors should be very cautious about and aware of what they're posting, particularly if certain videos can be perceived in different ways than intended. Get fellow team members' perspectives on the videos to balance fun content with professionalism. Since social media is global and part of your digital footprint, anything you post will remain forever. Be conscious of representing your organization well!

If you feel less comfortable directly posting content yourself, there's another way you can use social media for growth. Instead of investing in your personal marketing tactics, get those with established platforms to freely share your work. More specifically, consider creating a list of influencers, celebrities, and advocates who you know could be champions for your cause. Be *relentless* in cold-emailing individuals. I'd estimate that for every one hundred emails you send, you will hear back from ten. Pro tip: you can find a lot of famous people's emails in their YouTube bios! To increase your cold-contact success rate, diversify the platforms you reach out to: send Instagram messages and call influencers' agencies.

Another strategy for cold-contacting (influencers, partners, etc.) is to personalize each message so the other party knows what you admire most about them (aka do your research and pick people whose values match yours). Remember that on the receiving end of your email or message is a person; just like everyone else, they want to feel *seen*. Make a partnership or marketing endeavor mutually beneficial, rather than wording the message as a "Will you help me?"

Marketing your organization goes hand in hand with receiving press coverage and establishing partnerships. Getting national media coverage can entice a lot of supporters to reach out, while partnerships allow your organization to reach your partner's audience.

"Hey, Do You Want to Work with Us?"

Reaching out for partnerships can be scary. It's almost like asking someone out on a first date: you experience all the butterflies, nerves, excitement, and possibly . . . rejection. You put all of yourself out there and can only hope that they want you too.

Partners can come in the form of companies or organizations that donate funds, host joint events, market your initiatives, or increase the number of individuals you aid. If you're able to collaborate with a reputable and impactful organization or company, you are leveling up your nonprofit by association. Partners also offer new opportunities and resources.

To keep yourself and your team organized, I would recommend making a table of partners you want to reach out to, separated by category. Gather both phone numbers and email addresses. For most adults, they prefer, and answer more quickly, phone calls—as scary as that may be! Sometimes, to feel more confident, I'll prepare a script to read. Generally, my rule of thumb is to send two to three follow-up emails—spaced three to five business days apart—if I don't hear back from the company or organization. If it's someone I really want to work with, I'll even find other ways of contacting them, like through phone, LinkedIn, or social media.

TABLE 2: Partnership chart

POTENTIAL DONORS	EVENT OR PROGRAM COLLABORATORS	IMPACT (expand mental health access and suicide prevention)	MARKETING (spread awareness and reach LGBTQ+ youth)
• LGBTQ+ foundations • Mental health nonprofits • Technology companies	• Youth centers and shelters • School districts and LGBTQ+ clubs • Therapy platforms	• Schools and colleges (for early intervention) • Telehealth platforms • Nonprofits offering free/low-cost mental health care	• LGBTQ+ influencers • Media outlets (*Teen Vogue,* NowThis, *Vice*) • Social platforms with youth reach (TikTok, Snapchat)

Partners don't have to contribute only financially. Organizations and companies can support by offering expertise, volunteers, access to a target audience, and more. For example, a nonprofit working in LGBTQ+ crisis intervention might consider partnerships in the categories shown in table 2.

Don't rush the process of solidifying partnerships. Take the time to research each company and organization that you're reaching out to—noting their mission statement, values, and previous partnerships—so you can build the most robust partnership network possible. Assess their reputation, financial records, and ethical standards to ensure they align with yours. It can be smart to start out with smaller collaborations to test out the work dynamic before committing to a long-term agreement; everyone has different communication and organizational styles, so get to know your potential partners first!

To help you and your team get started on partnership outreach, write out ten to twenty companies in each category. For every company listed, focus on reaching out with a specific partnership request—brainstorming one to two ideas yourself instead of reaching out about a general partnership can convince more organizations to sign on. To successfully pitch a partnership idea, outline the mutual benefits each side would gain—brand visibility, shared impact, etc.—and tailor each email to the specific company or organization you are reaching out to. Discuss what you admire most about the expert or what the company/organization is doing. You can also frame the initial email almost as if you'd like to have a conversation rather than a give-and-take.

You can start with local organizations then work your way up to national and more well-known entities. This will get the ball rolling on scaling your organization and cementing your legitimacy in the non-profit space!

For small or new organizations, cold-pitching is a tried-and-true method for establishing partnerships—but don't overlook your personal network. Ask your team to comb through their contacts and log potential connections in a shared spreadsheet. Maybe someone knows a local business owner who could host a fundraiser or a family friend involved in a like-minded nonprofit. Personal connections will get you miles ahead of others!

Take Sreenidi's story with Code for All Minds. At just sixteen, she landed partnerships with major organizations like the National Education Association and Infosys Foundation USA. How? Through her connections. While interning at Connecticut's Commission on Human Rights, Sreenidi leveraged her relationship with her mentor to present her project to the Department of Education. That one connection led to meetings with twenty-plus professionals, a link to the lieutenant governor, and a partnership with Infosys's philanthropic division.

Sreenidi did send cold emails—but it was her network that ultimately opened doors and helped her scale her impact to thousands of students in under a year.

However, I understand that it's not always possible to have current connections already in place. In these cases, a strategy that I have found works really well is identifying and pursuing a target group. For example, if you're running a school composting program like Shrusti's Rise N Shine nonprofit, you may think about starting with one elementary school and using that school's success as a "case study" to spread the word about your program to other schools in the district and state. People underestimate the power of word of mouth, especially through professional networks! Focusing on securing one to five partners to eventually use as "case studies" to entice future partners to get on board with your organization is a smart tactic—particularly if you are starting from scratch. That way, you can point to them and say, "Hey, look, it works!"

An alternative to cold outreach online is attending in-person events that provide the opportunity to network with potential partners face-to-face. From conferences to school board meetings, you can scope out community events or meetings and make the effort to attend in order to build connections. For instance, if your goal is to increase equity in education, finding and attending education conferences can give you the chance to speak to educators, administrators, and experts that you would not have been able to engage with otherwise. Similarly, school board meetings can give you access to a network of leading directors in your county who can connect you with other important leaders. While it can be scary to take that step forward, placing yourself directly in front of a potential partner can help them assess the type of person you are and make it more likely for them to want to work with you. Plus, if you secure an email or LinkedIn after meeting in person (which you should always do to stay connected), you're able to follow up with a referral name in your email, rather than sending a completely cold email, to increase your chances of getting a response in your favor.

To get used to asking for partnerships or support in person, feel free to bring in a support buddy, like a friend or parent. Having someone there to feed you words of encouragement or back you up can make scary things like this a lot easier!

Your network is equivalent in importance to your nonprofit's net worth. Maintain consistent communication with your partners and support their initiatives to develop strong, long-lasting relationships. A good partnership can multiply your impact.

Getting Press to Tell Your Story

Press features provide nonprofits with a platform to reach wider audiences, which can translate into new volunteers, donors, team members, and supporters. Press can also help maintain current relationships by updating members about the organization's progress and new milestones. It's a great way to affirm the reputation of a nonprofit as well, which is particularly important for youth-led organizations. But, you may struggle to understand how to get press coverage. I know that as a freshman in high school, I didn't understand the best pitching strategies or how nonprofits even got their stories featured.

If you don't have connections with reporters, you want to start with cold-pitching to local news sites in your area. A statewide news site may possibly pick up on your organization and share the story with national news channels, spreading your message outward. The biggest thing to note about cold-pitching news organizations is that, more often than not, you will receive no response. I sent out over twenty emails and often heard back from only one—if any! Don't get discouraged—it is all part of the process and will help you develop strategies for what works.

CHECKLIST FOR COLD PITCHES

- ☐ It includes an eye-catching subject that's under nine words. (Reporters have so many emails . . . what will make them click on yours? Also, email subjects longer than nine words get cut off on a phone display screen, so try to keep the heading concise.)

- ☐ It uses bold statistics or details that discuss a recent event or achievement to draw the reader in. (Note that most reporters cover newsworthy events, so they won't often do a full feature on your organization, focusing instead on an event you're holding or a new award you've won.)

☐   It provides external links to a website, images, or social media.

☐   It includes background on your story. (Keep it concise and consider placing it as a "footnote" so readers can choose if they want to continue reading.)

Aside from cold pitches, there are platforms like HARO (Help a Reporter Out) and Qwoted that connect media and journalists with businesses and individuals. If you subscribe to their platforms every day, you will receive stories in your inbox that reporters are writing for various news outlets, from *Forbes* to smaller blogs. You can then send in a pitch, and if a reporter is interested in quoting you or in your story, they will reach out for more information.

Additionally, if you know other leaders or activists who have garnered national or international attention for their work, don't be afraid to reach out for pointers or even reporter contacts! I made new friends by doing this (shout-out to Rania—she leads LiTEArary Society, a nonprofit combating book deserts) and learned a lot about cold-pitching.

A more specific tip on how to successfully pitch to the press is to center your pitches on a recent local event your organization has hosted. Reporters generally want to cover timely stories that are relevant to their audience, so it makes more sense to share about the recent toy drive you did, for example, instead of the donation project you held last year. Also, if your pitch centers on a specific event rather than the organization as a whole, reporters will be more eager to cover it, since it creates a sense of urgency and conveys a concise, compelling narrative instead of broad organizational overviews. Just think about the news you read! You'll probably enjoy reading about an event with visuals, interviews, and other key moments more than a wider profile about a nonprofit.

Many news outlets also have specific reporters who cover human interest stories, community events, and local impact. Reach out to those reporters to cover your story because this increases the likelihood that they'll be interested in your pitch. For instance, it doesn't make much sense to pitch a story about this incredible climate change protest you held to a sports journalist; that's just a waste of your time and energy.

Press coverage isn't just about landing big media features—it can also spark a ripple effect. Alley-Oop, the youth-led sports nonprofit, demonstrates how local press can lead to national recognition.

Rishan and his team kickstarted their media journey by reaching out to local reporters who cover feel-good stories via Instagram and Facebook. After Alley-Oop installed a Lending Locker at a Richmond, California, high school, a local paper covered it. That article caught the attention of the Aspen Institute, which shared it in their newsletter and on social media.

Rishan followed up, thanked them, and asked about collaborating—which lead to a year-long partnership to create a Service Learning through Sports Toolkit. ESPN, an Aspen partner, noticed Alley-Oop's work and encouraged them to apply for the Billie Jean King Youth Leadership Award, which they won. The award brought in over $300,000 in funding and gear, plus coverage from major news outlets like NDTV.

Their journey shows that local press can be a powerful launchpad. By highlighting real community impact, Alley-Oop gained national recognition and formed lasting partnerships. Don't underestimate small outlets or overlook chances to follow up and build relationships—they can lead to something much bigger.

Here's Alley-Oop's example pitch email to the local Richmond newspaper:

SUBJECT: Teens Helping Richmond Soccer Team with Free Gear!

Hi Mr. _____,

I recently read your article, "Youth Soccer Team in Richmond Tries to Stay in Game," and was so inspired to help! ← *Shows the reporter that he reads and admires his work (personalization!).*

I am a high school sophomore, a total sports nut, and CEO of Alley-Oop Kids. Alley-Oop Kids is a kid-run nonprofit that has been helping level the playing field for underserved youth since 2014 and was even featured on Priyanka Chopra and Nick Jonas's Instagram stories for our work. ← *Subtle way to brag and slide in some cool details about Alley-Oop; big names like Priyanka Chopra also add an element of authenticity.*

I am writing because of our legacy project—the Alley-Oop Lending Locker. We install Lending Lockers at under-resourced schools and fill them with sports gear regularly through sports gear drives so that schools can share the gear with students. The lockers have taken off, and in just a few months, we have installed five lockers, including one in India, and are just trying to keep up with demand! On December 2nd, we will be installing a locker at Aspire Wilson Prep in Oakland. ← *Mentions the specific project the newspaper should touch on; bringing in specificity like this makes it more likely for the press to agree, compared to an overview article on Alley-Oop, since reporters want to cover relevant and unique events.*

We are in touch with Coach [NAME] to install a version of the locker at [SCHOOL IN RICHMOND] to fill their need for balls, uniforms, and other soccer gear ASAP, directly as a result of your article. Those kids should have a shot with the college scouts! ← *Why this newspaper specifically should cover Alley-Oop; they're directly impacting Richmond's community!*

Hoping you can help us spread the word about our lockers by covering this (and possibly our gear lending app coming soon)! Please let me know if you have any questions at all.

Your Press Persona

Once you land the opportunity to speak to the press, you want to think about crafting your press persona.

Now, don't worry; it's not like you're branding yourself as this whole new person or becoming some fictional comic book character. Adopting a press persona simply means crafting a press story that will communicate your nonprofit's brand to the world. This can look like identifying the specific details in your founding story that you want to highlight, the service programs that best represent the work you do, and the type of character you want to portray in interviews. If you've ever watched *The Hunger Games*, think of it like when Katniss and Peeta chose the theme of star-crossed lovers and "the girl on fire" in the game show. They executed their parts extremely well and dressed and acted in accordance with their chosen theme. In return, they earned more gifts because the audience believed in and fed into the personalities they conveyed. This is just like how present-day audiences and media give you more attention when you draw them in with a specific narrative or persona that is authentic to who you are, your values, and your convictions.

Once you start interviewing frequently with the press, you will recognize the questions that always come up: Why did you start your nonprofit? How do you balance it with your other commitments? What has been a favorite moment of yours? After realizing this pattern, I began keeping two to three stories in my back pocket that I could pull out when being interviewed. Similarly, you should brainstorm responses to common questions like these—and make sure your response is never over a couple of minutes to keep their attention—and rehearse them. Be sure to paint a picture with details and add emotion; doing so can help the media write better stories by adding context, giving your journey an angle, and demonstrating consistency across the work you do. In addition, always remember to thank the reporter or interviewer for covering your story. Journalists are overworked and often have to cover tons of topics at once. A thank-you will go a long way in building and maintaining relationships, and it's always nice to show appreciation!

7

The Ups and the Downs

RUNNING A NONPROFIT—like any ambitious endeavor—won't always be smooth sailing. You'll face failures, whether it's an event that flops, a grant application that gets rejected, or a partnership that falls through. At times, you may feel overwhelmed trying to juggle your nonprofit work with school, family responsibilities, and your personal life. You may even find yourself questioning whether you're capable enough to lead, especially when faced with self-doubt or criticism from others.

You've now done the work of building your nonprofit's identity, from the name and logo to the structure and why it matters. But behind every press feature or viral campaign is the *stuff that no one posts about.*

This chapter is for that part of you. We'll explore the messy, complicated, and *human* side of changing the world: how to manage failure with resilience, develop strong time-management skills to balance competing priorities, and stay motivated even when things get tough. We'll also tackle the emotional side of leadership—dealing with jealousy, self-doubt, and occasional negativity from peers. By the end, you'll have a road map for navigating the inevitable ups and downs of leadership, emerging stronger and more prepared for the journey ahead.

Falling *Forward*

Failure is inevitable and may even be the first challenge you encounter as a nonprofit leader. Maybe your first donation doesn't come through, or your social media campaign doesn't gain traction. But failure isn't just a setback—it's a learning opportunity. By developing the right mindset and tools to navigate failure, you'll build resilience and adaptability, making you unstoppable.

One of those tools is reflection. Reflection lets you process your actions and make necessary adjustments to flourish. For one, it enhances self-awareness. You will understand what drives you (to channel into greater success), your strengths (to capitalize on), your weaknesses (to understand what you can improve on), and your values (to guide your actions to align with your core principles). Second, as a leader, you'll encounter new experiences every day, whether that be navigating a workplace conflict or introducing a new product. By reflecting, you can analyze what went well and what didn't, allowing you to avoid making the same mistakes and improve your strategies. Last, reflection can increase your emotional intelligence. Leaders who reflect will begin to understand how their actions affect others, strengthening their ability to empathize. Thus, make it a habit to reflect daily, monthly, or after certain milestones (e.g., after winning an award, think about what you did well and why you think you received the award so you can replicate those same strategies moving forward—this also allows you to practice gratitude!).

Ways to reflect:

IMPLEMENTING A FEEDBACK SYSTEM: For instance, after every event hosted, send a survey asking participants to share criticism, or ask team members, friends, and mentors to share feedback on your performance.

KEEPING A JOURNAL: I like to write down daily journal entries to reflect on things that went well that day or things I struggled with. This can help you practice mindfulness and become more aware of your thoughts and emotions. This is particularly important when your organization goes through a challenging time. You can assess whether there are areas for growth for you and your team, which can help you take accountability and learn from your actions.

DESIGNING AND FILLING OUT A REFLECTION SHEET: My team usually designs our own reflection sheet with inspiration from Google or Canva templates. Usually, we jot down three things we do well, three things we want to improve, and three goals we have. Sometimes, during our quarterly meetings, we share our sheets to gain inspiration from each other.

SETTING ASIDE TIME. If you prefer a quicker and easier method, set aside five minutes when you wake up or before you go to bed to ask yourself reflection questions. Here are some good ones:

- "What went well today?"

- "What challenges did I face and how did I resolve them, or how should I resolve them?"

- "What can I improve on?"

- "What did I learn from this?"

However, I personally recommend writing down your reflections because you can look back at what you've thought through. Plus, it makes it easier to design action plans for future improvement.

Another tool is what I like to call the "tackle-one-with-three" method. Any time you fail at something—or encounter a setback—think of, write about, or say out loud three opportunities or positive things that you gained from that negative experience. This method works for both personal and career obstacles. For example, let's say you recently broke up with someone. The three positives could be (1) you now know what you *don't* want from your next partner, (2) you are free to meet the person you'll spend the rest of your life with, and (3) you gained back your time and personal autonomy. See how that can shift your perspective to an energizing and motivating force, rather than getting stuck in a limiting mindset?

Use this strategy every time you feel yourself giving up or losing hope. I always suggest writing down the three opportunities to internalize them and remind yourself anytime your mindset shifts back to a more negative perspective.

Tick Tock . . . Everything on Time Management

Juggling school, your nonprofit, family, and other outside commitments is *hard*. Adults tell me all the time how our generation of young people is doing ten times more extracurriculars than they ever could have. So, how can you do *everything* and still give your 100 percent?

In January 2021, Cancer Kids First volunteers skyrocketed from 120 to 7,000 in one week, thanks to a TikTok. Faced with the sudden growth, I was excited but soon became overwhelmed by managing such a large team. As an older sibling, I was used to hiding my imperfections to set an example. This limiting mindset transferred over to my leadership style (hello, founder's syndrome—more on that later).

I was unwilling to share my struggles. I pulled all-nighters, ignored my loved ones' concerns, and let school take a backseat. I'd stay up until 4 a.m. onboarding volunteers, sending out service opportunities, and answering hospital partnership emails. Every ping in my inbox gave me a hit of dopamine—I was on a high, and I didn't want to come down.

In CKF's early years, I was working nearly fifty hours a week on the nonprofit—while maintaining a 4.6 GPA, studying for the SAT, serving as student government president, joining nonprofit and startup leadership teams, mentoring other youth founders, interning for a senator, conducting research, swimming competitively, and helping care for my younger sister. Somehow, I still made it to every birthday dinner and hangout (I've always prioritized my friendships).

Eventually, my pre-calc teacher pulled me aside—my test grades had dropped from a 70 percent to a 30 percent. It was the wake-up call I needed. I realized I was running on fumes and neglecting everything else—including myself. I was sleep deprived, exhausted, and ignoring the people who cared most.

That moment forced me to hit reset. I started using time-management strategies that helped me balance my commitments and show up fully for everything I loved (and I pulled my pre-calc grade up to an A– by the end of the school year). Here are some of my favorite time-management strategies:

SETTING TIME LIMITS, TURNING ON DND, AND/OR REMOVING DISTRACTING APPS FROM YOUR HOME SCREEN: There are countless apps that allow your parents or friends to set a time limit on distracting apps on your phone (e.g., TikTok, Instagram, Snapchat, etc.). I just use the built-in time limit feature on my iPhone and allow myself one hour on each social media app per day. After that, I get a screen telling me I've reached my time limit on the app. The only downside is that I can hit "Ignore," which is why I sometimes remove the most time-consuming apps from my home screen so they're not just a click away. Turning on Do Not Disturb often works best for me, especially when I'm working on my laptop, because then I am not distracted by text notifications.

USING THE POMODORO TECHNIQUE: This technique from the 1980s was created by Francesco Cirillo, a university student who sought to master time management.[1] His recommendation was to set a timer and work for twenty-five minutes then take a five-minute break, but I tend to prefer working for an hour and taking a twenty-minute break or working for three hours and taking a one-hour break. The time intervals you pick can be up to you, but the main point is to give yourself a "work" time and a "rest" time for breaks. Also, I've found that every time I really want to go on my phone or watch Netflix instead of doing work, forcing myself to focus for five minutes gets my headspace back in the "lock-in" mindset.

TIME BLOCKING: This strategy may not work for everyone, but it is really helpful when I have a lot of different assignments to complete (e.g., chemistry homework, an English paper, an award application, and nonprofit tasks). Essentially, you estimate how long you will need on an assignment (e.g., one hour to finish the math problem set), set a timer in front of you for that amount of time, and complete your assignment in the allotted time. Once time is up, you have to move on to another assignment. The timer counting down places pressure on me to work as efficiently as possible, while forcing me to limit my distractions because I can't afford to lose time.

SCHEDULING: I can't overstate how much I love planners. I got my first one in third grade and haven't stopped using them since (my paper planner is basically part of my daily outfit). My friends can confirm how chaotic mine looked: every inch was filled. Over time, I realized that finding the *right* planner makes a huge difference in time man-agement. I've never liked digital tools like phone reminders—I need the satisfaction of physically crossing things off. My go-to in high school was always a Global Datebook with long daily columns. I had a whole system: pen for confirmed events and tests, pencil for tasks or tentative plans, and red pen to check things off. I even included little things like "text ___," "work out," and yes, even "shower" (I swear I remembered without it—I just liked writing *everything* down). My planner went *everywhere* with me. It wasn't cute—usually falling apart by the end of the year (shout-out to Zoe and Elina for teasing me and gifting me a new one), but it worked. My planner helped me stay organized, meet deadlines, and manage my packed schedule. Today, I use Google Calendar because of the convenience of setting up meetings through a digital calendar (and I average twenty-five hours in meetings a week). Find a format that works for you and build your own system because it makes all the difference!

UNDERSTANDING YOURSELF: I'll dive deeper into this, but I can't stress enough how important it is to know what you value most. For me, it's my relationships, so I've always prioritized time with friends and family. While my weekdays are packed with school and activities, I reserve Fridays through Sundays for loved ones. If I don't have time for full hangouts, I'll schedule study sessions or gym meetups to stay connected. I also learned that I'm most productive during the day, so I take nonprofit and internship calls before school, during lunch, or on my walk home. I built a routine based on my priorities: schoolwork comes first, then nonprofit tasks, clubs, or other extra-curriculars. I aim to stop working by 9 p.m. because that's when my energy dips. If you're more of a night owl, maybe you can save your harder assignments or studying for later in the evening. Adjust your work schedule to match what works best for you! I also need at least seven hours of sleep to function well, so unless I had weekend plans in high school, I stuck to a consistent sleep schedule—bed by 11 or midnight. Today, I wake up at 5:30 a.m. and go to sleep by 9:30 p.m. Some people, on the other hand, thrive on a few hours of sleep and a boost of caffeine. So, as the title of this tip suggests, understand yourself and your preferences and use that to your advantage!

When you're a student and you run a nonprofit, it's understandable that you have countless other commitments, whether it's working a part-time job or playing a sport. It can get overwhelming juggling all your tasks, so prioritization is key. If you have taken on the endeavor of founding a nonprofit, you must understand that you need to execute it well—because, not to put pressure on you, people's lives could depend on it! That being said, you cannot help others if you don't first take care of yourself. It's a cliché statement, sure, but sacrifice is a large part of running something of your own, and often, we are the first thing we sacrifice for our organizations.

Always remember to put yourself first and claim time as your own. Definitely take advantage of multitasking—whether that be balancing lunch with back-to-back meetings around town, writing essays on a flight, or doing your laundry while calling a coworker—but *never* sacrifice time for the things you want to do or the things you *need* to do for your mental health. Exercising, hanging out with friends, and even bed rotting are all activities you shouldn't put yourself down for partaking in. Diana Chao, the founder of Letters to Strangers, put it beautifully: "Why do we always have to grow at the cost of ourselves, when sometimes maintaining what we have is the toughest, most important thing of all? [I tell myself that] the world keeps turning, even when I rest—*especially* when I rest. It gives me the space to dream of a better future."

While you're knee-deep in running your organization, remind yourself that your physical and mental health are key to not only your well-being but also your organization's. Never forget to take downtime or spend time doing things you love.

Get a Move On!

Something else you may struggle with is facing obstacles like hundreds of unanswered emails or rejections of partnership requests.

In times like these, finding ways to motivate yourself will carry you forward. The most effective strategies can depend on your personality, but here are some of my favorite motivational strategies that got me through those tough times:

CREATING A VISION BOARD—ONLINE OR HANDMADE: I have a digital "career-centric" vision board on my laptop so that I am reminded of my dream future each time I work, and a 2025 "everyday life" vision board that I hang in my room with my general life goals (see figure 3). The visualization aspect of vision boards and the ability to see them every day keeps me on track and pushes me toward what I envision for myself.

SETTING MINI GOALS: In addition to a vision board, create a list of SMART goals. SMART stands for

> ▸ Specific (think about who, what, where, when, and why)

> ▸ Measurable (how will you determine if you've met the goal?)

FIGURE 3: 2025 vision board.

> ► Achievable (do you have the tools/skills to achieve the goal, and if not, how will you acquire them?)
>
> ► Relevant (does your goal align with your broader aspirations?)
>
> ► Time bound (make sure you have a target date for achieving all your goals)

I like to set SMART goals each year in three categories: school, CKF, and personal growth. Breaking my goals into categories helps me stay focused and balanced. While I haven't always hit every goal perfectly, setting clear, intentional targets has consistently helped me make meaningful progress.

BUILDING A "WORDS" FOLDER: This is by far my favorite motivational tip: I have a folder in my camera roll filled with screenshots of emails, DMs, and texts I've received from peers, patients' parents, partners, mentors, and strangers detailing how I've helped or inspired them in some way. Whenever I'm feeling self-doubt or struggling to work, I look back at this folder to remind myself of the impact I've already had and the potential I have moving forward. There's truly nothing like reading words from someone you've impacted.

REWARDING YOURSELF: During college application season, my mom and I went out to eat every time I was accepted into a top school. Celebrating your accomplishments is crucial for motivating yourself to achieve your goals. Psychologically, your brain will be wired to work toward achieving them because it knows you'll receive something pleasurable at the end of the journey. It's similar to how a dog trains itself to pee outside because it knows its owner will give it a treat for doing so.

ESTABLISHING AN ACCOUNTABILITY SYSTEM: While peer pressure tends to carry a negative connotation, it can actually be helpful at times too. Sometimes, when I set a goal for myself, I ask a friend or parent to hold me accountable in achieving it. When the deadline I set inches closer and I still haven't made progress, they step in and pressure me to complete it. For your organization's goals, having a codirector or work colleague place a bit of peer pressure on you can give you that burst of motivation you need.

PRACTICING GRATITUDE: If you know me, you know that I'm big on gratitude. Every night before I go to bed, I think about three things I am grateful for that happened that day. I also love journaling in my gratitude journal. Practicing gratitude, in the long run, can help you live a happier and more satisfying life. It can also shift your mindset, allowing you to see opportunities rather than focusing on the negatives.

FINDING ROLE MODELS: Role models can be great motivators, especially in our digital age, as we can easily access information and updates about their lives to give us that extra kick to get started. My biggest inspiration has always been Sophia Kianni—*And I got* *to put her in this book!!! How cool is that*—because of the path she is paving for women of color in the social activism and nonprofit space. She is a visionary who relentlessly fights for what she believes in, tackles cool projects, and maintains her pure heart and personality. I know stalking someone's social media can be considered toxic and negative for one's mental health, but I would argue that, like peer pressure, when used in the right way, social media "stalking" can be helpful. Going through her Instagram and reading about the speeches, events, and projects she has undertaken inspires me about what my next goals should be and shapes my steps forward. Find people you admire online or around you, and look to them for motivation.

Jealousy, Judgment, and Everything in Between

Starting something of your own and putting it out into the world is scary. When I first launched Cancer Kids First, I kept it mostly to myself. My close friends were incredibly supportive. They helped distribute flyers for our first toy drive and shared our fundraising link with everyone they knew. But some people from my high school community didn't respond with that same encouragement. Classmates and their parents whispered about how I only started CKF to "get into college" and doubted my true intentions. What they didn't know—and never asked—was the story behind why I started CKF and the emotional toll it took on me to build it.

These strangers knew nothing about my life, yet they assumed everything. Parents of students from the grades below reached out to my parents, asking, "Who did you pay to grow CKF?" Peers asked, "Your dad made the website, right?" Someone even asked if my mom, who works at a nonprofit, used her connections to get CKF off the ground. When CKF became the world's largest youth-led cancer nonprofit, these same parents then asked me to help their children start nonprofits . . . funny how that works, isn't it?

In reality, my family immigrated here with nothing. We grew up on food stamps, and my clothes and furniture came from thrown-out items on the sidewalk. My parents worked nonstop just to keep us afloat. I didn't even tell them about CKF for the first three months because I didn't want to stress them out.

This hurdle was perhaps the most difficult personal challenge I faced, because other people's assumptions meant that five years of my blood, sweat, and tears had been reduced to nothing in an instant. I felt like I had to somehow prove *over and over again* that I deserved everything I had worked for *because I had worked so hard for it*. I cannot count the number of times I pushed myself to the brink of burnout trying to show these doubters that CKF was truly something my team and I had created on our own.

It took me a long time to find peace in the face of this judgment. A close friend of mine, Peyton, once told me: "You should only care about what the people who love you think. Strangers' words don't and shouldn't matter—they don't know you." That line has stayed with me ever since. Whenever I hear rumors or feel the sting of someone minimizing my work, I remind myself that the people who matter—my family, my childhood teacher, my grandfather—*know* what I put into this. That's what counts.

You can't change what other people think of you, but you can save yourself the mental struggle of doing so by finding comfort in knowing *who you are*. Follow and uphold your values to become the best version of yourself that you can be. To help you reinforce your sense of self, you can create something tangible—like a memory box—that includes keepsakes of mini successes from the founding of your organization or mementos that remind you why you started in the first place. Speaking affirmations in the mirror (e.g., "I am powerful and capable") also helps, even if it feels awkward!

Eventually, I realized that a lot of these assumptions stemmed from others' jealousy and insecurity. It reminded me of the quote, "Someone who hates you normally hates you for one of three reasons. They either see you as a threat. They hate themselves. Or they want to be you." I didn't believe it until high school, but I could suddenly feel a shift as CKF began growing. People were suddenly very aware of who I was, as I was also student body president, had won several leadership and academic accolades, and had a big group of friends because I loved connecting with people. Tension rose to new heights during college application season. A friend told me, "You were really well-known in school . . . and I think when you're that known, it's easy for people to hate you because you're so conveniently there *to hate*."

Rumors started flying. A girl I'd known for years—someone I had literally helped with college essays and student government elections—told people I only got into Harvard because I "networked my way there." Another girl asked me to withdraw my Ivy League application because I was "taking her spot." At first, I thought she was joking. Then she asked again. And again. When I got in and she didn't, she flipped. I was even called a "nepo baby" by a classmate who refused to believe that I started CKF on my own and insisted I "stole" it from someone else.

I've always been a bit of a people pleaser, so knowing that people didn't like me—especially based on lies—was painful. But experiencing jealousy early on taught me an important lesson: *you cannot let other people's bitterness dictate how brightly you shine.*

People can project all they want. But while they waste energy trying to tear you down, you're growing, improving, and pursuing your goals. They're focused on you because they're not focused on themselves.

Whenever jealousy starts to wear me down, I go back to my support system. I journal. I remind myself of what I've built. And every time I invest in my happiness, my circle becomes more positive, supportive, and genuine.

The Likability Dilemma

After a while, you'll realize that not every difficult person in your nonprofit journey is outwardly negative. Some may be subtle or genuinely mean well. But even then, you'll find yourself constantly trying to keep everyone happy—team members, mentors, donors, strangers on the internet—and letting their opinions affect your decision-making abilities. It's what I like to call the "likability dilemma." It's a tightrope walk between assertiveness and approval, and it can wear you down if you don't name it and navigate it early.

The likability dilemma has been studied in countless leadership scenarios because it heavily influences our leadership style and results, even if we don't notice it. Alice Eagly and Linda Carli, two social psychologists known for their work on gender and leadership, call this phenomenon the "double-bind theory," as women, and especially women of color, are caught in a "double bind": if they are assertive, they're seen as unlikable.[2] Yet if they're warm, they're seen as ineffective or "not leadership material." The double-bind theory applies to young leaders too, who may be told to "tone it down" or "wait your turn."

In fact, I have experienced firsthand adults diminishing my leadership capabilities due to my age, gender, and race. In my senior year of high school, I applied for a full-ride scholarship for community service leaders. I became one of the finalists, and all that was left was an interview. That day, I was nervous but excited to present who I was to their admissions committee. I had done numerous practice-round interviews and felt prepared to impress.

My interviewer was a thin white man who was around his late fifties. He seemed nice enough. We fell into a nice routine as he began asking questions and I responded with detailed stories. However, the interview took a turn when he asked about a personal challenge I had faced within my family. I got emotional—as any sixteen-year-old might when speaking about something traumatic—and tears welled up. It wasn't a full-on breakdown; I just needed a moment to collect myself. Still, I felt embarrassed at the time. The interviewer's response only amplified that feeling: "Good leaders don't cry," he said. That comment stuck with me. I left the interview in a low mood, and my principal and biggest mentor, Dr. Reilly, quickly caught on. She sat me down and asked me what had happened, and after I shared how stupid I felt for "screwing everything up with my emotions," she told me that the way the interviewer had treated me was wrong. Female leaders are denounced because men claim we are too "emotional." However, Dr. Reilly reminded me that my emotions aren't a hindrance; instead, they are something I can capitalize on to propel myself and my work. Looking back, I see my emotion not as a weakness, but as a reflection of how much I cared. And frankly, his reaction says more about his outdated idea of leadership than it does about me.

While I didn't end up getting the scholarship, I look back on that moment to remind myself of my strengths. When I feel things, I feel things deeply, and I use those powerful emotions to drive the work that I do. There's something magical about that, and no man (or woman) should ever try to make me feel bad for *feeling*.

I am extremely lucky to have the most exceptional adults, like Dr. Reilly, and friends in my life who not only support me in countless ways but also uplift me and are there for me in times of need. A few months later, Dr. Reilly even organized a mock interview for me with a few of my school's administrators to prepare me for another scholarship I had applied for (I did end up getting that one, and I really owe it all to her).

The failed scholarship interview was an incredible learning experience for me. It conceptualized how leaders of color and female leaders are more likely to face social or professional penalties for exhibiting dominant or ambitious behavior yet are condemned as leaders if they display vulnerability. This societal norm is wrong and leads to emotional labor: managing not just your work but also others' reactions to your tone, body language, and personality. For young, female, and BIPOC leaders, the **emotional labor** is amplified. Understanding this helps you reject unfair or discriminatory responses without allowing them to define you. Leadership isn't about being universally liked. It's about being respected, being clear on your values, and showing up with consistency and heart.

In fact, it's pretty common for leaders starting out to believe that their goal is to make their community happy. This is false. Your mandate is to understand your target group, from its needs to its dynamics, and transform it for the better. Strong leaders understand that not all decisions they make will initially satisfy all parties, but the end result is for the betterment of the community as a whole.

Through the years, I developed a five-component plan to make decisions without the influence of others:

1. COLLECTING DATA: In short, get the facts. All of them. Whether it's a partnership decision or a fight between directors, get both sides of the story (and don't rely on "he said, she saids") before making a decision. Sometimes, I like to use the five Ws (who, what, when, where, and why) to collect all the appropriate information.

2. COMMUNICATING: I can't stress enough how important it is to communicate with your team. Most decisions you make as a leader will impact a wider audience than just yourself. Keep all parties updated and involved in the situation.

3. AGREEING TO DISAGREE: You're not going to end up agreeing with everyone about your decision. What you must do, however, is believe in the choice you're making (see why the "collect data" step is so important?). Professionally stand your ground when it comes to your decisions because you are a *leader*, not a cheerleader.

4. OWNING UP TO THINGS: Even though you must stand your ground, you also have to recognize when you might be at fault. Take accountability for any mistakes or wrongdoings you might have made in the decision-making process. And as a leader, you are not only responsible for your own words and actions but also for those of everyone on your team as well.

5. KEEPING YOUR HEAD UP, SHOULDERS BACK: While some of the decisions you make will clearly have a right answer, others may be more muddled. Time and experience will help make the decision-making process easier, but for now, keep a level head during the backlash and decompress in private.

A general rule of thumb is to trust yourself on vision and values, but trust others on their specialty. If someone knows more about finance, design, or outreach, remember that you brought them on for a reason . . . and that reason is not to just follow you! Leaders must practice integrity and accountability. Upholding strong ethical principles will build credibility and respect within your team. When you admit your mistakes and hold yourself accountable, your directors and team members will follow suit. Know how to straddle the line between standing up for yourself and acknowledging a mistake. While you won't get it perfect every time, you'll learn to ground yourself in purpose, not popularity.

Your Backbone and Support System

Throughout this book, I've emphasized the importance of surrounding yourself with the right people. While building a strong nonprofit team is essential, having a solid support system in your *personal* life is just as crucial for your growth as a leader.

Think about the closest people in your life and the ones that you interact with every day: your family, friends, classmates, teachers, coaches, and mentors. Your attitude, personality, and beliefs are largely shaped by those around you; if you spend 24/7 with an overly negative person, you're more likely to develop a negative mindset yourself. That's what makes your circle so important.

Everyone needs "comfort humans"—those who truly get you, share your values, and offer steady support when you need to vent or decompress. But you also need people who challenge you, who tell you the hard truths, and who push you to grow. And finally, you need people who inspire you—those miles ahead who can teach you what you don't yet know. If you have one person in each of those categories, you're already in a great place.

Ensuring that you surround yourself with the best people requires conducting what is called the "values exercise." The following list was inspired by ideas from College Essay Guy, who uses the values exercise for college essay brainstorming.[3] However, I think it's equally applicable to determining what types of people you want in your life.

Pick five values that resonate most with you. These five values are what you should look for in your friends and mentors. They can also be used to reevaluate some friendships that may not be benefiting you (this doesn't mean just cutting people off, but this reflection exercise is a great way to build a better social circle). For instance, one of my top values is "inspiration," meaning that my closest friends all inspire me to be better in some way, whether that's through their academic work ethic or their courage to try new things.

PERSONAL GROWTH AND CHARACTER

- Accountability
- Courage
- Wisdom
- Authenticity
- Growth
- Purpose

RELATIONSHIPS AND CONNECTIONS

- Love
- Trust
- Compassion
- Respect
- Communication
- Empathy

CAREER AND MOTIVATION

- ▸ Leadership
- ▸ Success
- ▸ Meaningful work
- ▸ Productivity
- ▸ Inspiration

LEARNING AND EXPLORATION

- ▸ Knowledge
- ▸ Curiosity
- ▸ Creativity
- ▸ Social change

WELL-BEING AND VALUES

- ▸ Health
- ▸ Peace
- ▸ Gratitude
- ▸ Honesty

Aside from meeting people and creating a support system organically, you can also create an intentional network through outreach (I'm sure you can sense how important cold outreach is by now!). Sophia Kianni built an inspiring network of fellow Stanford students, climate advocates, and business executives by reaching out to school professors and teachers, searching on LinkedIn, and cold-emailing people to create a mentorship network. Her network has driven her work not only with Climate Cardinals but also with the fashion startup, Phia, that she started with Phoebe Gates.

Think about seeking connections who are not only professionals in the field of your choice but also students! Always remember that there is no shortage of learning opportunities out there and that to be a good leader, you must yearn to learn more and continuously improve yourself. If you're the strongest person at the table, you're sitting at the wrong table.

Embracing diverse leaders from all backgrounds and ages can shape your future for the better. Not only can you learn from others' knowledge, but you can also pick up on their habits, lifestyle choices, ways of thinking, and behaviors. We truly are the average of the five people we spend the most time with.

8

Measure It, Scale It

YOU'VE NOW BUILT AN ORGANIZATION that is *real*. You've learned to lead with purpose, overcome setbacks, and serve your community authentically and passionately.

This final chapter is about growth with *intention*. Whether you're launching your nonprofit's second year or just trying to figure out what success really looks like, this chapter will help you measure what matters. We'll talk about outcomes, impact, and how to scale without losing your heart.

As your nonprofit grows, consider how you can scale your impact beyond your local community and develop deeper roots. Could your programs be replicated in other regions? Is there a way to collaborate with national or international partners to expand your reach? Thoughtful, strategic growth ensures that you're not just reaching more people but are truly making a difference in their lives—wherever they may be.

Measuring Impact

With all the facets of running a nonprofit organization, it can be easy to get caught up in other objectives. However, your primary goal should be to create the greatest impact as defined by your mission statement and programs. Reflect back on why you started your nonprofit. What was your biggest dream? Where do you see your organization in a year? In five years? What areas are you and your team excelling in? What areas need improvement? Consistently setting goals based on reflection is crucial for evaluating the success of your organization and identifying potential areas for growth.

Without measuring impact and checking in on its effectiveness, you and your team may be pouring time and energy into initiatives that could be better spent elsewhere. For example, when Lea from Beauty Beyond Bars spoke directly with incarcerated individuals who had received donations from her organization, their feedback led to meaningful changes in how services were delivered. Her target group opened up about how while the donations were an immediate solution to an immediate problem, after the donations were used up, the issue of proper hygiene in America's criminal justice system remained. BBB's donations could only do so much.

Lea reflected on these comments and conducted background research on more sustainable solutions to help her target group. She discerned that passing legislation to mandate the toiletries she had been donating would create a deeper systemic change. Thus, BBB added a second prong to their service focus: supporting the enactment of policies to humanize living conditions behind bars.

Without taking the time to speak to her target group, Lea could have never understood the transformative impact policy had on the people she was trying to help. Doing the necessary data collection gave her nonprofit greater insights into how best to make a difference. Data can guide decisions.

Now, how do you even get started with quantifying impact? Identifying KPIs, or key performance indicators, is a common way to measure results. This could be output indicators (number of volunteers or number of items delivered), outcome indicators (increase in skills or knowledge), or impact indicators (decrease in homelessness or improvement in water quality by 30 percent).

KPIs turn actions into measurable progress. It's easy to say "We helped people," but KPIs show *how many, how well,* and *what changed*. Additionally, KPIs go a long way in making your nonprofit fundable and credible. Grants often ask for success metrics to determine whether you're passionate and have potential.

One of my favorite ways to measure impact is through questionnaires, surveys, or interviews. After an event, reach out to beneficiaries and participants to gather feedback. But ensure surveys are well-designed, as poor construction can lead to biased or misleading results. For example, you might only hear from people who had an extreme experience—positive or negative—while most others stay silent. That's why it's crucial to think intentionally about *who* you're asking, *how* you're asking, and *what* you plan to do with the data. Or you can choose a timeline (e.g., every quarter) to send out feedback forms. You can explore this option both in person and virtually through platforms such as Google Forms, SurveyMonkey, or Excel. Analyzing your final quantitative data (how many lives were impacted?) and qualitative data (how did XYZ feel afterward?) can lead to deeper insights. For example, Letters to Strangers conducts pre- and post-workshop surveys with the same questions so that they can compare the change in answers about mental health knowledge after their curriculum. Moreover, they use a mix of clinically evaluated wellness survey indicators after every event that are unique to their programs and the local cultural context. On a more regular basis, Letters to Strangers will collect qualitative interview-based stories and insights from individual members and audiences to understand their experiences and needs in greater detail. This feedback loop ensures they stay on track and adjust as necessary.

After measuring impact, communicating your findings in the form of an impact report, social media post, or website feature can be a great way to show your stakeholders and supporters the progress your organization has made. While it's not legally required or mandated, it's smart to share them to prove your organization's value. Using the impact data you collect for future decision-making can also propel further growth.

The Paani Project, which builds wells for communities in need, prioritizes impact transparency with their donors in an innovative way. Sonny knew that there were a lot of organizations already working on the water shortage issue, but something they did not do well was making the process transparent. After donating money to the organizations, people didn't know what happened to their contributions. They saw no physical product that came out of their monetary donation, disincentivizing them from donating again. Sonny came up with a solution to this problem by measuring, then sharing, Paani Project's impact.

Sonny productized the wells: through package pricing of $200, $600, or $650, people can buy wells for themselves or as a gift in honor of someone else so that people can drink water in their name. After every donation, Sonny and his team give the donor access to a Google Drive folder with photos of the well's construction process, the plaque with the donor's name on it, and people drinking from the well. Beneficiaries see the impact of their money in ninety to one hundred days (three to four months). This creative way of measuring and sharing impact brings Paani Project's supporters into the impact experience itself, adding value to their lives. They are more likely to donate again or even refer a friend because it is extremely transparent where their money is going. In fact, as of 2024, the Paani Project has constructed 20,000-plus wells.

As Sonny's project demonstrates, to continue the cycle of donations and support, you should document your nonprofit's impact and share it with current and future donors. Bring them into your organization's process and acknowledge their contributions. Great things can come from that!

National and International Impact

Generally, most successful nonprofits start with helping a small group of people in their surrounding community to get a feel for how their organization should run and to grasp their target audience's needs. Later on, organizations can expand nationally or even internationally.

Zoe Terry, a now eighteen-year-old, founded Zoe's Dolls at the age of five. Her organization is a great example of how a series of quiet signals, rather than a singular "Aha!" moment, can entice a nonprofit to expand nationally and internationally. Zoe's Dolls focuses on girl empowerment and antibullying through a variety of programs and events that incorporate fitness, self-expression, community spirit, and empowerment. Particularly, the nonprofit unites the community in donating new dolls of color to give out to little girls in need. Zoe's Dolls originally centered on supporting little brown girls in the United States. After operating nationwide for four years, media attention enticed Zoe to expand outward. She received countless emails from passionate students abroad who wanted to start chapters or help out their home countries. What she had thought was a problem only in the United States was exacerbated tenfold in other countries, broadening her perspective on global political and cultural climates.

Zoe immediately began googling and reaching out to like-minded organizations and programs in countries like Haiti, Zambia, and Cuba to donate dolls. Since founding her nonprofit, she has given out over 60,000 dolls worldwide.

Similar to Zoe's Dolls, you can research international organizations in your field once you feel you are ready to extend your impact globally. You can also think about how your organization fits into your daily life: if you're traveling abroad, see if you have the opportunity to reach out to your target audience in that country (e.g., when Zoe did a summer study abroad program in Greece, she looked for opportunities to give out dolls to local organizations that were supporting refugees). Consider stepping outside of being a "traditional tourist" when you visit another country in order to embody global citizenship. Take a minute to research the climate of the country you're going to visit. Understand the culture and the people and keep your eyes open for opportunities to help others. This is especially important if you are traveling to a developing country, as there may be social, political, and environmental concerns that are pertinent but are uncommon in your home country.

Saawan's nonprofit, LiteratureDiversified, is another organization that exhibits thoughtful and organic national growth. When Saawan first launched LiteratureDiversified, it was a local effort to push for racially inclusive curricula in Texas classrooms. But once they piloted several lesson plans, teachers from other states started reaching out about their lesson plans through mutual connections and social media. Numerous student leaders also reached out asking, "Can I bring this curricula to my school?" That organic interest told Saawan that their model was scalable because it was adaptable.

Saawan's advice to other youth leaders is this: expand when *pull exceeds push*. Don't force national growth; instead, notice when demand naturally outpaces your current capacity. If people outside your immediate network are asking to join, or if you find yourself repeatedly customizing resources for different contexts, that's a sign you're ready to scale. But scale intentionally. Expansion is about infrastructure, not just numbers. Before LiteratureDiversified grew nationally, Saawan made sure he had the right systems in place: a clear volunteer onboarding process, adaptable curricula, and regional leads to keep the organization community-specific and targeted. Saawan emphasizes that the key to recognizing that growth doesn't mean taking on more alone; it means building a framework so others can lead too. Trust your instincts, but also listen to your team. If they're ready to carry the mission forward, that's your green light.

Next-Gen Leadership

As Saawan's journey hinted, the greatest lesson you will learn about true leadership is that the best leaders cultivate and uplift others to become leaders themselves. This is why the best companies and organizations host leadership training to lift up their employees internally. This maintains a lasting legacy and gives you the ability to carry your impact further to national and international levels.

Cultivating leadership can seem abstract: How can you tell if you've done it well? What methods can you even take to begin such a thing?

At the start of founding an organization, it can be easy to fall into the pattern of micromanaging. You may want to design the website, post on social media, plan events, coordinate with partners, create a five-year timeline, and manage a team of directors. However, all good leaders must come to realize that delegating tasks is an important part of demonstrating trust in your team and a way to give them opportunities. By taking everything on yourself, you are inhibiting your team members from growing as directors. There's even a name for it! Founder's syndrome refers to a common organizational challenge that occurs when the founder of a nonprofit (or startup) struggles to let go of control or adapt to the organization's growth and evolving needs.[1] Founder's syndrome usually stems from deep commitment to the formation of the organization, so it's not inherently bad, but it can hinder the organization's ability to scale, professionalize, or empower other leaders.

With a micromanaging CEO, your directors are not given the autonomy to make their own decisions or handle their own projects, which is something leaders do. Make sure you're showing your employees that you trust them by handing them challenging projects they can tackle with your guidance. It'll stretch their skills, give them a chance to lead, and build your relationship with them. Plus, when you give them the space to share about their work in team meetings, you're handing them ownership and a sense of responsibility for the work they're doing.

Another prime way to cultivate leadership is to acknowledge those around you, both privately and publicly. Our TikTok director, Layla, taught me this lesson during a phone conversation we had about a newspaper interview I had recently completed. I had gushed to the reporter about how amazing our success on social media was but never mentioned the work Layla had put in to get us there. Layla's call was a reality check. It was as if blinders had been removed; I never realized how little I was crediting important members of our team until that moment. From then on, I ensured that I mentioned the names of the team members who played a vital role in the creation of Cancer Kids First and invited our leadership team to live interviews or calls to tell the press their own stories.

Other ways to acknowledge team members include annual awards for the best director (or other methods of rewards/prizes), so they know you see it when they go above and beyond, as well as small forms of praise like "I am so proud of you" and "What you did was awesome!" Often, I'll text in our main leadership group chat when a director has done something well (to uplift that team member and inspire others) or even post the accomplishment on social media. It doesn't even always relate to work; I've congratulated our directors for committing to college and winning their sports game before! We all want to be seen and heard; make sure your directors know you care about them (in and out of the workplace) and want to see them succeed.

From an outside awards perspective, you can nominate qualified team members for social impact accolades you think they deserve. These can include the Points of Light service award, the Diana Award, the Presidential Volunteer Service Award, and more. Once again, giving your team members the space to be acknowledged for volunteering their time and energy can help you retain them and provide further opportunities along their leadership journeys.

Because I believe heavily in the power of reflection, my nonprofit's HR managers and I work together to make evaluation and reflection sheets for our team. This gives them all the opportunity to practice reflection on their own leadership and gives our main officer team insight into how we can improve the work we do for them. Our amazing HR managers also share inspirational quotes related to leadership in the group chat to empower our team members and foster a positive team environment. This cultivates a space where our team can grow individually and collectively.

Finally, workshops and mentorships can be critical to cultivating other leaders. You can invite professors, board members, CEOs, motivational speakers, and other leaders to conduct workshops or training sessions for your team. Ask your team who they would be interested in hearing from. These workshops can give your team members new connections and strong role models.

Consider opportunities like Awareness 360, a nonprofit cofounded by Shomy Chowdhury and Rijve Arefin that equips young people with leadership and project management skills to raise awareness about global issues. Over four months and twenty expert-led sessions, participants learn about the UN Sustainable Development Goals and engage in peer discussions. After the program, fellows implement their own impact projects with support such as needs assessments and potential travel grants.

Fellowships and incubators like Awareness 360; Three Dot Dash, which connects teen leaders with industry experts; and TRIIBE, which offers funding and mentorship to college sophomores scaling nonprofits, provide invaluable training, community, and guidance to help emerging changemakers grow.

Outside of leadership and service development, you could also provide mentorship to your team's directors by fostering general professional growth. Take the time to sit down with each team member, or poll your leadership team as a whole, and learn about each member's goals. Maybe they are in the midst of applying for internships, in which case you can support them by sharing résumé and interview advice. You could also connect them with professionals in their field of interest.

CONCLUSION

IF YOU'VE MADE IT TO THE END, congratulations! That means you're not just interested in social impact. You're serious about it. You've taken the time to understand how to build something meaningful from the ground up: identifying a problem, designing a solution, building a team, sustaining your mission, and navigating every unexpected challenge in between. And now, you are equipped with the foundational tools and mindset to launch and lead a 501(c)(3) nonprofit as a young person.

Let me be clear: this journey won't be easy. Nothing in this book was meant to oversimplify the path ahead. As you've probably noticed, fundraising can be discouraging, and leadership can feel isolating. Strategic decisions may sometimes leave you feeling torn or struggling to stay authentic to yourself. You'll encounter ethical trade-offs, pressure to grow fast, moments of impostor syndrome, and the harsh reality that even with your best efforts, you can't solve everything. But that doesn't mean you aren't making an impact. In fact, that's what real changemaking looks like—wrestling with complexity, listening deeply, and continuing to show up anyway.

If you are a committed and passionate leader with a growth mindset, I wholeheartedly encourage you to start something of your own. Building a nonprofit as a young person pushes you to lead with empathy, communicate clearly, adapt constantly, and learn fast. It expands your worldview and your capacity to care—not just about issues, but about people. You'll meet individuals who will shape you. You'll travel to places that shift your perspective. And most importantly, you'll grow into a version of yourself that you never imagined possible.

I can't fully put into words everything I've gained from running Cancer Kids First, from the lessons to the relationships, but it made me who I am. From delivering speeches to students across the country to collaborating with international nonprofit leaders, this work has opened doors and deepened my commitment to service in ways no classroom ever could.

I hope this book gives you not only direction but also permission to take yourself seriously, to trust your ideas, and to lead as YOUth. I hope it reminds you that while injustice is real and heavy, so is your potential to fight it. You don't have to wait for a degree, a job title, or a perfect plan to begin.

And as you go forward, absorb every moment. Appreciate the people around you. Say yes to things that scare you. Make mistakes, reflect, and keep going. Consider passing this book to someone else who has the potential to bring light to a community. And, above all, support the young people around you, who, much like yourself, are pushing to transform the world—one step at a time. **YOUth = more powerful when united**.

I'm so proud of you, and even more excited for the journey you are about to embark on. Share your journey with me and stay connected! *oliviazhang.net* | *@oliviazhangofficial*

With love and belief in you,
Olivia

TOOLBOX FOR CHANGEMAKERS

Legal Forms

Legal forms are often the most daunting part of starting a nonprofit. If you're anything like me (a humanities lover), tax forms and legal jargon can seem foreign. When I started Cancer Kids First, I spent hours figuring out what forms to file and when. Taking time to plan your organization's mission, vision, and team makes the process much smoother.

Some organizations apply for 501(c)(3) status right away. Others host a few events first (like a donation drive or fundraiser) to build support before formalizing. There's no "right" path, just pros and cons to each.

Note: Legal requirements and costs vary by state. Starting a nonprofit can also be pricey; CKF paid about $400 to $600 in 2019, so raising initial funds may help.

Before filing for 501(c)(3) status, you need to

1. Elect at least three unrelated adult directors. Choose mentors who can help your nonprofit grow—think teachers, executives, or trusted family friends. One must serve as your registered agent, the legal point of contact for your nonprofit who receives government notices and legal documents.

2. Choose your tax year. You'll pick between a calendar year (January 1 to December 31) or a fiscal year (any twelve-month period ending in a month other than December). Once selected, this year will be referenced in key documents like your bylaws, EIN application, Form 1023, and Form 990. This decision also determines when your nonprofit's annual government forms—like Form 990—are due.

3. Register your nonprofit with your state.

4. Adopt bylaws (your nonprofit's internal rules).

5. Apply for an EIN (employer identification number)—your nonprofit's version of a Social Security number.

The following are step-by-step instructions to incorporate your organization with the state and federal government.

STEP 1: FILE ARTICLES OF INCORPORATION (~$75).

This legally establishes your nonprofit in your state. Steps and required documents vary, so check your state's specific instructions on the IRS's "State links for exempt organizations" web page.

Be sure to include the required language to qualify for tax-exempt status and provide your nonprofit's name, address, and registered agent details. Your state's nonprofit formation packet, if available, most likely includes the articles of incorporation, bylaws, and organizational minutes.

Bylaws aren't submitted; they are internal. They outline your board structure, voting rules, and meeting frequency. Approval of articles typically takes about a month.

STEP 2: APPLY FOR AN EIN.

This process is the quickest and easiest of all the government forms; you can apply online through the IRS website under "Apply for an employer identification number online."

STEP 3: FILE FOR 501(C)(3) STATUS.

Most youth-led nonprofits qualify for Form 1023-EZ, a simplified online version of the federal tax-exempt application. Check the IRS eligibility worksheet to be sure your nonprofit qualifies.

Some states require separate applications for state tax exemption. In other states, federal approval automatically triggers state exemption. Check with your state tax agency to confirm the process.

STEP 4: PURSUE ONGOING RESPONSIBILITIES.

Filing doesn't stop once you're official—you'll have annual legal requirements to maintain tax-exempt status. Having a treasurer or CFO to manage finances and compliance can help.

- Complete the IRS Form 990-N ("e-postcard"), which is for organizations with less than $50,000 in receipts. This takes ten minutes and requires only eight basic pieces of information:

  1. Employer identification number (EIN), also known as a taxpayer identification number (TIN)

  2. Tax year (calendar or fiscal)

  3. Legal name and mailing address

  4. Any other names the organization uses

  5. Name and address of a principal officer

  6. Website address if the organization has one

  7. Confirmation that the organization's annual gross receipts are $50,000 or less

  8. If applicable, a statement that the organization has terminated or is terminating (going out of business)

  The purpose of this form is to make the use of your organization's funds transparent, thereby retaining your current donors and attracting new donors. If your revenue is less than $200,000, you may file 990-EZ. If your revenue is more than $500,000, you'll file the full 990 form.

▶ State-specific forms may be required to fundraise legally. For example, Virginia's Form 102 costs $100–$425 based on financial history, while smaller nonprofits can file a simpler Form 100 for $10.

Missing deadlines can lead to late fees—or worse, the loss of tax-exempt status. If you fail to file Form 990-N three years in a row, your nonprofit will automatically lose its tax-exempt status.

Set up reminders in your calendar and planner, and hold an official board meeting to adopt bylaws, elect officers, and approve filings. Keep meeting minutes in a binder for future reference.

Legal forms can feel intimidating—but you don't have to do it alone. If you can afford it, hiring a lawyer ensures accuracy and saves time. Otherwise, tap into your network! CKF's board member Jo Moak had legal experience and helped guide us through filings, copyright questions, and policies for in-person events. Her help was crucial, especially early on.

If you don't know a lawyer, consider reaching out to one to join your board. Many professionals are happy to support causes they care about, and some may offer pro bono services. For example, Soraya Johnson, founder of UNITE! Woman in Need, received help from local attorneys who donated their time.

Banks

Opening a bank account is an essential step for youth nonprofit leaders—not just for managing money, but for establishing credibility, accountability, and growth potential. However, minors cannot legally open business bank accounts on their own in the United States. To work around this regulation, you can either have an adult cosigner (usually a parent or board member) or form a 501(c)(3) with an adult listed.

Table 3 is a chart of banks that work well for youth-led nonprofits.

TABLE 3: Bank chart

BANK	YOUTH-FRIENDLY FEATURES	NOTES
Bank of America	Online banking; debit cards	Requires an EIN and adult signer
Chase	Strong digital tools	Need adult on account
Capital One	No-fee options for nonprofits	Not all branches support business accounts
Bluevine	No monthly fees; virtual card	Must be eighteen-plus (adult signer or board member needed)
Local credit unions	Often more flexible with youth	Great for local organizations with smaller budgets

NOTES

CHAPTER 1

1 "60+ Key Nonprofit Statistics: Essential Insights for 2024," *Philanthropy News Digest*, March 31, 2024, *https://philanthropynewsdigest.org/news/other-sources/article/?id =14803735&title=60+-Key-Nonprofit-Statistics:-Essential-Insights-for-2024.*

2 Julia Kagan, "501(c)(3) Organizations: What It Is, Pros and Cons, Examples," *Investopedia*, last modified March 24, 2024, *https://www.investopedia.com/terms /1/501c3-organizations.asp.*

CHAPTER 2

1 Kendra Cherry, "Intrinsic Motivation vs. Extrinsic Motivation: What's the Difference?," *Verywell Mind*, last modified July 26, 2023, *https://www.verywellmind.com /differences-between-extrinsic-and-intrinsic-motivation-2795384.*

2 Michael Feder, "What Is an Elevator Pitch?," University of Phoenix, last modified December 1, 2023, *https://www.phoenix.edu/blog/what-is -elevator-pitch.html.*

3 Julia Hanna, "Power Posing: Fake It Until You Make It," *Working Knowledge* (Harvard Business School), September 20, 2010, *https://www.library.hbs.edu /working-knowledge/power-posing-fake-it-until-you-make-it.*

CHAPTER 3

1 . "About Us," *Feeding America*, accessed June 16, 2025, *https://www.feedingamerica .org/about-us.*

2 "Fundraising Talking Points," American Red Cross, accessed July 26, 2025, *https:// www.redcross.org/content/dam/redcross/donations/p2p-livestreaming/Quick_Glance _Fundraiser_Talking_Points-General.pdf.*

3 "Who We Are," Cancer Kids First, accessed June 16, 2025, *https://www.cancerkids first.org/.*

CHAPTER 4

1   "Brands," Restaurant Brands International, accessed June 16, 2025, *https://www.rbi
.com/English/brands/default.aspx.*

CHAPTER 5

1   "Women of Worth," L'Oréal Paris USA, accessed June 16, 2025, *https://www
.lorealparisusa.com/women-of-worth.*

2   "The Princeton Prize in Race Relations," Princeton University, accessed June 16,
2025, *https://pprize.princeton.edu/.*

3   "About Rise," Rise, accessed June 16, 2025, *https://www.risefortheworld.org
/about-rise/.*

4   "About Us," Gloria Barron Prize for Young Heroes, accessed June 16, 2025, *https://
barronprize.org/about-us/.*

5   "Ambition Accelerator Goes to India: Inaugural Summit Recap," Taco Bell Foundation, October 1, 2024, *https://www.tacobellfoundation.org/ambition-accelerator
/ambition-accelerator-goes-to-india-inaugural-summit-recap/.*

6   "What You Need To Know about Commercial Co-Ventures," GlobalGiving, June
26, 2018, *https://www.globalgiving.org/learn/commercial-coventure.*

CHAPTER 7

1   "The Pomodoro Technique—Why It Works & How to Use It?" *Replicon*, January 2,
2023, *https://www.replicon.com/blog/pomodoro-technique/.*

2   Alice H. Eagly and Linda L. Carli, "Women and the Labyrinth of Leadership," *Harvard Business Review* 85, no. 9 (September 2007): 62–71, 146, *https://hbr.org/2007
/09/women-and-the-labyrinth-of-leadership.*

3   "The Values Exercise," College Essay Guy, accessed August 15, 2025, *https://www
.collegeessayguy.com/blog/the-values-exercise.*

CHAPTER 8

1   "Founder's Syndrome Undermines the Legacy of Strong Leaders," *Cranfield Trust*
(blog), April 26, 2022, *https://www.cranfieldtrust.org/articles/founder-syndrome
-undermines-the-legacy-of-strong-leaders.*

ACKNOWLEDGMENTS

THIS BOOK EXISTS because of the extraordinary people in my life. I'm lucky beyond words to be surrounded by people who lift me up when I fall, call me out when necessary, push me to be the best version of myself, and celebrate every win like it's their own. I would not be here today without them.

To my mom, the most dedicated and loving person I know—thank you for being my greatest role model. Your unwavering support, sharp instincts, and tireless belief in me have shaped every part of who I am. From brainstorming strategies to sharing your leadership lessons, you've shaped how I lead with both empathy and excellence. You were CKF's very first donor, and I'll never forget it.

To my dad and my sister Ava, thank you for showing your love in practical and profound ways. Whether collecting CKF donations or checking in from afar, you made sure I was supported, even when I didn't ask.

To my best friends—Zoe, Saira, Nadia, Elina, Emily, Gaby, Jason, Della, Anna, Amani, Bianca, Tessa, Nashla, Bahar, Elaine, Peyton, Kritika—you showed me what true friendship means. You were there for the deep conversations and the hidden breakdowns. You believed in me before I believed in myself. You cared for me when I was sick, volunteered when I was shorthanded, provided a second opinion whenever I needed it, and never stopped cheering me on. You dealt with my crazy schedule, sat through my mid-conversation Zooms, and stood by me when I was overwhelmed. Your love carried me through my lowest moments and shaped me into someone stronger and endlessly grateful.

To Ellen Reilly, my high school principal—thank you for teaching me to lead with courage and for providing me with opportunities to fulfill my potential. You helped me navigate doubt and discrimination and reminded me that I could rise above it.

To the past and present CKF leadership team and volunteers—thank you for believing in our mission and giving it your all. Your dedication and creativity have powered everything we've built. I'm constantly inspired by your heart and commitment.

To Ms. Handy, Ms. Donoghue, Ms. Nightingale, Ms. Bao, Ms. Rosario, and Ms. Hill—your guidance shaped how I think, write, and lead. You gave me the tools and confidence that I still lean on today. To Sandra Buteau and Dana Bryson—thank you for giving a student a seat at the table and trusting my voice in rooms of adults.

To Rita Rosenkranz, my literary agent, and the entire Berrett-Koehler team—thank you for taking a chance on me when I was still finding my voice. You opened doors I once only dreamed of. To Jeevan Sivasubramaniam, my brilliant editor—thank you for seeing this project's potential from the start and for guiding me with patience and insight. You challenged me, and I'm better for it.

And to every person, organization, and community that believed in me and lent a hand—thank you. My story is shaped by yours, and I hope to one day pay it forward by mentoring the next generation of dreamers, just as you did for me.

INDEX

NUMBERS

16 Personalities (MBTI) quiz, 52
501(c)(3)
    bank account for, 41
    legal status, 6, 123, 125
    tools to launch, 121
    types of, 14–16

A

accomplishments, celebrating, 100, 118
accountability, 100, 106, 107
activism
    forms of, 7–9
    passion for, 12
    personal experience for, 13–14
adaptation/change
    learned via mistakes, 92
    to mission/service programs, 36
    to new nonprofit model, 16
administrative expenses, 40
adults, underestimation by, 20, 22
advisers. *See* mentors
advocacy, policy-based, 35
affirmations, positive, 26, 102
age. *See* youth

agreeing to disagree, 106
AI, name help from, 30
Alley-Oop, 36, 37, 86–87
Amula, Shrusti, 21, 51, 82
Anderson, Sawyer, 73
annual budgeting, 38–39
app creation, 8
apps, removing distracting, 95
Arefin, Rijve, 119
articles of incorporation, 124
asks, specificity of, 23
assumptions/judgment, 101–102
audits, financial, 41
authentic self, 27
awards, 70–73, 86, 118
Awareness 360, 119
awareness/advocacy nonprofits, 14, 16, 34

B

Bala, Sreenidi, 20, 82
bank account, dedicated, 41–42, 126–127
Bank of America, 41
Basilico, Matthew, 74
Beauty Beyond Bars, 9, 16, 29, 112

Bhimaraju, Sriram, 15
Billie Jean King Youth Leadership
    Award, 86
Bizri, Layla, 79, 117–118
board of directors, 38, 53–55, 123
boldness of youth, 19
bonding, team, 61, 63
Born This Way Foundation, 35
branding
    and calls to action, 78
    for marketing, 77–80
    press coverage, 84–87
    press persona, 88–89
    of you and your story, 77
budget creation, 38–39
burnout, 46
business vs. personal life, 44–46
bylaws, 124

C

calendars, 96
calls to action, 78
campaigns, fundraising, 73–75
Cancer Kids First (CKF)
    acknowledging team of, 118
    early fundraisers for, 68
    experience that initiated, 1–3, 101
    founding days of, 25, 44–46
    growth of, 77, 94
    original mission of, 34
    problem addressed by, 11
    projected budget for, 39
    time required for, 94
Canva, 31, 93
care gaps, identifying, 12
Carli, Linda, 104
causes, researching, 34–35
celebrating accomplishments,
    100, 118
CEO/president, 46–47, 65

CFO/treasurer, 47
challenges
    judgment of others, 101–103
    learning from, 93–94
    likability dilemma, 104
    motivation to face, 98–101
    reflection about, 92–93
    ups and downs of leadership, 91
changemakers
    age as asset for, 17
    awards for, 72
    future generations of, 3, 116–119
    tools for, 2, 123–127
Chao, Diana, 23, 98
chapter director, 48
charitable organizations, 5, 6, 9, 69
ChatGPT, name help from, 30
Chowdhury, Shomy, 119
Climate Cardinals, 28, 109
Code for All Minds (CFAM),
    20–21, 82
cofounder, choosing a, 49–50
cold-messaging
    increasing success rate for, 79–80
    for marketing, 79
    to potential partners, 82
    of potential team members, 50
    for press coverage, 84–86
    support network via, 109
communications director, 47
communication with team members,
    50, 63, 106
community mapping, 13, 16, 34, 35,
    112
community outreach, 83
community projects, 5
compromise, to resolve conflict,
    60–61
concise mission statements, 33
confidence, 25, 26–28

conflict, navigating team, 60–65
connection, human, 74, 107–110
connections, partners via
    personal, 82
COO (chief operations officer), 47
COVID pandemic, 12, 13, 37, 70
creativity with service programs,
    34, 35
crowdfunding, 73

D

data collection, 106
data-driven approach, 21
decision-making tips, 106–107
decompression, 107
designing the logo, 31–32
Diana Award, 118
digital calendar, 96
digital natives, 20, 73
disengagement, 74
Doctors Without Borders, 14
donation nonprofits, 14
donations
    asking other groups for, 69
    business partnerships for, 69
    donation drives, 36
    to other organizations, 42
    See also funding/fundraisers
double-bind theory, 104
Dunbar, Robin, 74
Dunbar's number, 74
Duvvuri, Saawan, 56, 116

E

Eagly, Alice, 104
ego, leadership and, 65
EIN (employer identification
    number), 124
elevator pitch, 21–24, 68, 69
email, sample pitch, 54

emotional intelligence, 92
emotions, overwhelm by, 104–105
empathy, 63, 74
energy of youth, 67–68
energy/time requirements, 10, 34,
    94–98
ethics, code of, 107
events director, 47
Excel tools, 39
expenses, income and, 38–39, 41

F

Facebook, 86
failure
    as inevitable, 92
    learning from, 25, 92
favoritism, avoiding, 46
fear
    of difficult conversations, 63
    facing your, 26
    freedom from, 28
    of fundraising, 68
    of rejection, 25
feedback
    from the community served, 34
    constructive, to team, 46
    implementing system for, 92
    to measure impact, 112, 113
    via surveys, 113
Feeding America, 33
financials
    annual planning of, 38–39
    awards, 70–73, 86
    budget creation, 38–39
    foundation for, 37–42
    as publicly accessible, 7
    tax reporting, 40–41
    transparency about, 114
    See also funding/fundraisers
firing team members, 64–65

flexibility
    amid inevitable changes, 37
    of mission statements, 34
Ford Foundation, 14
Form 990 filing, 36, 40, 125, 126
founder-market fit, 10
freshness of youth, 19
friends, working with, 44–46
funding/fundraisers
    campaign crafting, 73–75
    energy/drive for, 67–68
    fundraising expenses, 40
    local fundraising, 68–69
    national fundraising, 69–70
    and nonprofit legal status, 6
    one-time, 7, 13
    partners for, 81
    via personal connection, 74, 77
    small-scale, 67
    transparency with donors, 114
Fundly, 74
fundraising nonprofits, 15
future, the
    changemakers of, 3
    as inherited by young people, 19

G

Gates, Phoebe, 109
Gen Z digital natives, 20
Givebutter, 74
GivePulse, 78
global challenges
    activism to address, 7–9
    lack of empathy with, 74
    prevalence of, 1
Global Datebook, 96
Gloria Barron Prize for Young
    Heroes, 72
goals
    brainstorming, 11

    to create impact, 111–112
    financials for, 38
    of service programs, 32–37
    setting mini, 98
    vision boards, 98
GoFundMe, 70, 73
GoFundMe Pro, 74
Gomez, Selena, 35
Google Ads grants, 70
Google Calendar, 96
grant director, 48
grantmaking nonprofits, 15
grants, 70–73
gratitude practice, 100
grief, 1, 10
growth, organizational, 111, 116
growth, personal, 107, 121–122
Guo, Natalie, 12, 70
gut instinct, 63

H

HARO (Help a Reporter Out), 85
home/work separation, 46
honoring loved ones, 10–11
hormones, reducing stress, 24

I

idea generation
    AI for help with, 30
    passion as driving, 11
    scalable ideas, 37, 58, 116
Idealist, 78
impact, knowing your, 99–100
impact, measuring your, 111–114
incarcerated community, 9
income and expenses, 38–39, 41
industry professionals, 53–55
Infosys Foundation USA, 82
in-kind events, 69
insecurity of others, 102–103

Instagram, 95, 101
Instagram Reels, 23, 78, 86
integrity, personal, 107
Internal Revenue Service, 32, 36, 40,
    124, 125
international impact, 115–116
internships, 66
interviews, 88

J
jealousy, 101–103
Johnson, Soraya, 126
Jordan, Michael, 43
journaling, 92
judgment/assumptions, 101–102

K
Kendra Scott, 69
Khan, Sonny, 31, 114
Kianni, Sophia, 28, 52, 100–101, 109
KPIs (key performance indicators),
    112–113

L
labor, emotional, 105
Lady Gaga, 35
leadership
    benefits of youthful, 18–20
    confidence and, 26–28
    conflict navigation and, 60
    decision-making by, 106–107
    delegation by, 117
    development of, 58
    double-bind theory in, 104–105
    facing tough situations in, 64–66
    female leaders, 104–105
    inspiring next gen, 116–119
    learning from mistakes for, 25
    likability dilemma in, 104
    management vs., 24

reflection and, 92–93
steel and velvet style of, 62
team, 38, 43
ups and downs of, 91
of your peers, 43
legal forms, 123–126
Lending Lockers, 37, 86
Letters to Strangers, 23, 35, 98
Leukemia & Lymphoma Society, 15
LGBTQ+ crisis intervention, 81
life, separating business and personal,
    44–46
likability dilemma, 103–104
LinkedIn, 24, 50, 53, 80
LiTEArary Society, 85
LiteratureDiversified, 56, 116
lobbying, 8, 34
local fundraising, 68–69
logos, 11, 29–32
long-term considerations
    in elevator pitch, 22–23
    while starting up, 13
L'Oréal Women of Worth, 72

M
management vs. leadership, 24
marginalized groups, 104–105
marketing, 77–80, 81
memory box, 102
mental health, 23, 35, 81
mentors
    for future changemakers, 3
    inspiration from role models, 100
    and next-gen leadership, 117, 119
    partnerships via, 82
    via social impact awards, 71
    support from, 21, 104–105
    within teams, 59–60
    values shared with, 108
micromanaging, 117

mindset
  for changemaking, 18
  leadership, 24
  from limited to growth, 93–94
minimization of your work from
  others, 102
mission
  financial integrity and
    commitment to, 40
  impact in line with, 112
  of partner organizations, 81
  statement, 32–37, 55
  team members' support for, 49
  volunteers to support, 56
mistakes
  as inevitable, 92
  learning from, 25, 92
Moak, Jo, 126
motivation
  feelings as driving, 105
  loss of, 61–62
  from role models, 100–101
  tips for sustained, 98–101
  values to guide, 109

N

name, nonprofit, 29–32
National Alliance on Mental
  Illness, 14
National Education Association, 82
national fundraising, 69–70
national impact, 115–116
needs assessment, 34, 35
Nepomuceno, Lea, 9, 29, 112
networking, 83
nonprofits
  alternatives to, 5, 7–9
  defined, 5–6
  finances for, 6, 37–42
  gaps from other nonprofits, 35

global statistics on, 5
initial events/service programs,
  36, 37
long-term considerations, 13
measuring impact of, 111–114
mission iteration for, 37
passion to sustain, 12
press coverage for, 84
reasons to start, 7, 9–10
role of volunteers in, 56–57
scaling, 52
as tax exempt, 5–6
team positions for legal, 46–47
tools to build, 2
types of, 14–16
understanding mandate for, 106
note-taking, 11
NSHSS scholarships, 72

O

Obama, Barack, 25
Off Their Plate, 12, 70
output/outcome indicators, 112
outreach director, 47

P

Paani Project, 31, 114
partners/partnerships
  assessing potential, 11
  with businesses to raise funds,
    69, 73
  mutual benefit for, 80
  outreach for, 80–83
  via personal connections, 82
  with the press, 88–89
  reaching new audiences via, 80
  rejections by potential, 25
passion, loss of, 61–62
passion to sustain work, 12, 22, 43,
  49, 51, 56

Patel, Rishan, 37, 86
PayPal donation pools, 70
peers
    accountability among, 100
    building team from, 50–51
    community of, 50
    educating your, 35
    leading your, 43
    motivating your, 18
    support from, 109–110
persona, press, 88–89
personal experience
    with conflict navigation, 60
    in fundraising campaign, 74
    leadership as built via, 24
    learning from vulnerability, 105
    referenced in elevator pitch,
        22–24
    responses to, 10–11
    of team members, 49
personal time, 97–98
personal vs. business life, 44–46
Phia, 109
pilot events, 36
pitches
    cold pitches to press outlets,
        84–86
    for fundraising, 68, 69
    honing elevator pitch, 21–24
    to potential partners, 81–82
planners/scheduling, 96
podcasts, 8
Points of Light, 78, 118
Pomodoro technique, 95
positive affirmations, 26, 102
power hours for donations, 70
power pose, 23–24
president/CEO, 46–47
Presidential Volunteer Service
    Award, 118

press coverage, 84–87
Princeton Prize in Race Relations, 72
problems, unaddressed
    assessing viability to serve, 10–14
    data-driven approach to, 21
    as founding reason, 9
    international, 115–116
    mission statement and, 32–33
    partners in serving, 81
    in personal sphere, 20–21
    researching/understanding,
        34–35
program costs, 40
projected budgets, 38–39
protests, organizing, 8
public charities, 6
purpose, turning grief into, 1
putting yourself out there, 80–83

Q

Qwoted, 85

R

Rare Beauty fund, 35
reflection, self-, 92–93, 108, 118
registered agents, 41
Reilly, Dr., 104–105
rejection, fear of, 25
relationship-building, 88, 107–110
researching causes, 34–35
resilience, 92
respect, likability vs., 105
responsibility, taking, 106
rest, 98
Restaurant Brands International, 66
retention, team member, 53, 58
right-hand person, tips for choosing,
    49–50
Rise Fellowship, 72
Rise N Shine, 21, 51, 82

role models, 100
roles, team, 46–47, 56

S

salience, 74, 75
Sathyanarayanan, Nidhi, 48
scalable ideas, 37, 58, 116
scheduling, 96
scholarships, 72
school, juggling, 95, 97
school clubs, 7
schools, marketing at, 78
Seas Brighter Foundation, 15
secretary/COO, 47
self, authentic, 27, 102
self-care, 97–98
self-doubt, 28
self-love, 27
service-based nonprofits, 14, 41
service programs, 32–37, 81
shyness, 25
slacker behavior, 61–62
SMART goals, 98–99
Snapchat, 95
social change advocacy, 15, 17,
    34–35
social impact awards, 71
social media
    campaigns, 8, 23
    cold-messaging on, 79–80
    distraction by, 95
    fundraising via, 70, 73
    leadership team on, 59
    marketing via, 78–79
    reporting your impact on,
        113–114
    research on, 78–79
    team application on, 52
    team member shout-outs on, 58
social media director, 47

social network, 107–110
specificity in fundraising efforts,
    74–75
specificity in mission statement, 33
spending, tracking, 40
status, desire for, 65
status quo, challenges to, 1, 17
steel and velvet leadership, 62
storytelling, for your brand, 77,
    88–89
stress, reducing, 24
support
    from board of directors, 55
    elevator pitch to drum up, 21–24
    and feedback, 34
    rallying from mentors/
        community, 21, 34
    teamwork and, 48
    from volunteers, 56
    in your personal life, 107
surveys, 113

T

"tackle-one-with-three" method,
    93–94
Taco Bell Ambition Accelerator, 72
tax code, US, 5–6
tax-exempt status, 5–6, 32–33, 40,
    123, 125
tax reporting, 40–41, 124, 125–126
team
    for 501(c)(3) status, 123
    acknowledging your, 117–118
    application for potential, 51–52
    board of directors, 53–55
    building team culture, 58–59
    communication with, 50
    delegating to, 117
    financial transparency with, 37
    firing members of, 64–65

growth motivated by, 116
ideas for structuring, 11
interviewing potential
    members, 52
leadership team, 38, 43, 50, 59
leading your, 27
mentorship within, 59–60
navigating conflicts on, 60–65
organization for, 80
passion shared by, 51
positions for foundational, 46–47
professionals on, 53–55
reflection by, 93
roles and expectations for, 56, 59
social media posts by, 79
tips for selecting members of,
    49–50
virtual connection for, 58
volunteer teams, 58
working with friends, 44–46
technology, knowledge of, 20, 73
Terry, Zoe, 115
Three Dot Dash, 119
Thrive Capital, 12
TikTok, 23, 78, 79, 94, 95, 117
time blocking, 96
time management, 94–98
tourism, intentional, 115–116
tracking expenses, 40
transparency, 114
treasurer/CFO, 47
trends
    vs. meaningful issues, 12
    mission pivots and, 37
    understanding social media, 78
TRIIBE, 119

U

underserved populations, 14
UNITE! Woman in Need, 126

UN Sustainable Development
    Goals, 119

V

values, prioritizing your, 96–97, 108
virtual events, 36
virtual movie nights, 70
virtual raffles, 70
vision boards, 98
vision statement, 55
volunteer director, 47, 48
volunteers
    assessing, 57
    community support by, 7
    growing base of, 78
    for local fundraisers, 68
    roles for, 56–57
    as team members, 51
vulnerability, 105

W

walk-a-thons, virtual, 70
Water Works, 73
WEGO Health, 2
well-being, prioritizing your, 98, 109
Wellspring for the World, 73
workshops, holding, 36, 119
World Child Cancer USA, 2
World Vision, 73
World Wildlife Fund, 14
writing
    activism via, 8–9
    mental health support via, 23
    nonprofits based on, 35

Y

youth
    vs. age-based credibility, 17, 20
    bank accounts for minors, 41–42
    benefits of, 18–20, 67

youth (continued)
   as a changemaking asset, 17
   double-bind theory for, 104
   energy of, 67–68
   minimization based on, 104
   youth-centric grants, 71

YOUth: The Young Person's Guide to Starting a Nonprofit (Zhang), 1

Z

Zhang, Olivia, 1–2
Zoe's Dolls, 115

ABOUT THE AUTHOR

OLIVIA ZHANG is the founder and CEO of Cancer Kids First, the world's largest youth-led nonprofit supporting children with cancer. Since launching the organization at age fourteen, she has mobilized over 40,500 volunteers across eighty countries and delivered over $600,000 in donations to pediatric patients. As the youngest recipient of the 2025 L'Oréal Paris Women of Worth award, a recipient of the 2023 Diana Legacy Award, and the youngest-ever WEGO Health Top Patient Leader, Olivia has been featured by *People*, CBS News, and TEDx. She currently studies economics and global health at Harvard University and is passionate about empowering the next generation of changemakers.

Berrett-Koehler
PUBLISHERS

Dear Reader,

Welcome to the Berrett-Koehler Community—a global network of changemakers creating positive impact in their lives, organizations, and communities.

Our Mission: Connecting People and Ideas to Create a World That Works for All

We believe transformation is possible. While outdated paradigms of self-interest, exclusion, and hierarchy continue to hold back our communities and organizations, we know that change can happen. That's why we connect people with actionable ideas from leading experts who are already creating the solutions we need.

The BK Way

We're an independent publisher that practices what we publish. Our books, digital resources, and community offerings provide practical pathways for building more just, equitable, and sustainable organizations and lives. Whether you're transforming your workplace, community, or personal practices, our publications meet you where you are with tools that work.

But we don't just talk about positive change—we live it. Through "The BK Way," we put stewardship and purpose before profit. As a benefit corporation, we're legally committed to benefiting all our stakeholders: authors, readers, employees, communities, and the environment.

As our gift to you, claim your free bestselling ebook at bkconnection.com/welcome. You'll also receive fresh leadership insights delivered to your inbox from bkconnection.com/blogs/the-bk-exchange.

You Make the Difference

We're grateful to our readers, authors, and community members, who bring our mission to life every day. Your stories of transformation inspire us and show others what's possible.

Share how BK publications are making a difference in your world at bkconnection.com/impact.

Your friends at Berrett-Koehler

Join the Berrett-Koehler Community

Are you passionate about supporting independent publishing and reading diverse voices and perspectives? Join the BK Community Membership Program and become a part of a vibrant literary community. To support mission-based publishing while saving up to 30 percent on all books and attending exclusive events, visit ideas .bkconnection.com/bkcommunity-join to learn more and become a member.